ROUTLEDGE LIBRARY EDITIONS:
THE ECONOMICS AND POLITICS OF OIL
AND GAS

Volume 4

OIL IMPERIALISM

OIL IMPERIALISM
The International Struggle For Petroleum

LOUIS FISCHER

Routledge
Taylor & Francis Group

LONDON AND NEW YORK

First published in 1927 by George Allen & Unwin Ltd.

This edition first published in 2016
by Routledge
2 Park Square, Milton Park, Abingdon, Oxon OX14 4RN

and by Routledge
711 Third Avenue, New York, NY 10017

Routledge is an imprint of the Taylor & Francis Group, an informa business

British Library Cataloguing in Publication Data
A catalogue record for this book is available from the British Library

ISBN: 978-1-138-64127-3 (Set)
ISBN: 978-1-315-62232-3 (Set) (ebk)
ISBN: 978-1-138-65566-9 (Volume 4) (hbk)
ISBN: 978-1-315-62235-4 (Volume 4) (ebk)

Publisher's Note
The publisher has gone to great lengths to ensure the quality of this reprint but
points out that some imperfections in the original copies may be apparent.

Disclaimer
The publisher has made every effort to trace copyright holders and would welcome
correspondence from those they have been unable to trace.

OIL
IMPERIALISM

The International Struggle
For Petroleum

BY

LOUIS FISCHER

LONDON : GEORGE ALLEN & UNWIN LTD.
RUSKIN HOUSE, 40 MUSEUM STREET, W.C. 1

PREFACE

This manuscript was written in Moscow, Berlin, London and New York on the basis of information and material collected in those capitals. I wish to use this opportunity of expressing thanks to Herr Dr. Zeeck, chief of the archives of the German Foreign Office and to A. E. Vorobyov, the librarian of the Soviet Commissariat for Foreign Affairs, who placed interesting and valuable data at my disposal, and to the officials and oil men in various countries, whose opinions and knowledge, when they shared them with me, were of considerable assistance.

Except where they are explicitly marked in the text as originating with Bolshevik spokesmen, statements on Soviet policy rest on my own conception of it. In each case, however, I have been guided by interviews with Russian officials, by some understanding of Communist tactics and psychology, by a study of Soviet periodicals and documents, and by impressions gathered in Russia between 1922 and 1925.

Several documents reproduced in whole or in part have never been published. Likewise, some facts relating to concession negotiations in Moscow and elsewhere have hitherto been secret.

I am especially grateful to Frederick Kuh, Berlin correspondent of the *United Press*, whose encouragement in the early stage of the work helped me to carry it to a close, and to Freda Kirchwey, the Managing Editor of *The Nation*.

LOUIS FISCHER.

New York, March, 1926.

CONTENTS

CHAPTER   PAGE

     PREFACE 5

     INTRODUCTION 9

I. THE WAR FOR BAKU 19

II. THE GENOA CONFERENCE AND OIL . . 38

III. IN THE ROYAL DUTCH CAPITAL . . . 68

IV. THE OIL BLOCKADE AND AFTER . . . 92

V. STANDARD OIL BACKS RUSSIAN RECOGNITION 109

VI. SOVIET CONCESSIONS 150

VII. THE UNITED STATES, JAPAN, AND RUSSIA 174

VIII. IN THE SHAHDOM OF PERSIA 208

     CONCLUSION 237

     BIBLIOGRAPHY 247

     INDEX 251

INTRODUCTION

The best proof of the importance of Russian oil is the efforts of the Powers and the powerful oil trusts to get hold of it. If the petroleum resources of Mosul first shape military campaigns in the World War, then precipitate a serious diplomatic crisis between the United States and Great Britain, and subsequently almost involve Turkey and England in active hostilities despite the fact that their extent is still unknown and that one London expert has volunteered to drink all the oil that is discovered there, it is not difficult to imagine the lengths to which nations and oil magnates would go in order to acquire the petroliferous lands of Baku, Grosni, Emba and Maikop in Russia—lands which contain as much oil as will be found anywhere under a single national flag.

Oil has fomented revolutions in Mexico, unseated a series of presidents in that republic, and brought hostile armies to and across its borders. Yet there is more petroleum in the Caucasus than in Mexico. Persian cabinets have fallen, Persian parliaments have been dissolved, an American consul has been killed, loans have been refused, State Departments have grown green with anger, on account of the North Persian oil-fields where not a single barrel of liquid has been mined. How much more diplomatic commotion, financial manœuvring, political disturbance, military activities, and loss of life must the oil kings feel themselves justified in causing for the sake of the Russian oilfields which have been producing for more than a century and whose underground stocks are surpassed by those of no country, not even of the United States.

It is quite as hazardous to estimate the underground oil reserves of a given patch of oleous territory as it is to guess the quantity of gin a child in swaddling clothes will swallow by the time it is grey and rheumatic. The statistics of geological surveys, the evaluations of mining engineers and the exaggerations of patriots on this point can only serve purposes of orientation; they are never more than relative. Yet everyone who dabbles in this dangerous realm of judging the volume of the dark green-brown rivers which flow unseen hundreds of feet below the earth's surface invariably gives Russia a place quite near the top of the list of countries.

L. M. Fanning, of the American Petroleum Institute, for instance, says of Russian oil resources that they are "as great or greater than those of this country" [1] (the United States), and other experts are of a similar opinion. Then we have the view of G. Lomov, the president of the Russian Naphtha Syndicate, who believes that "in the matter of underground resources, the Soviet Union occupies first place. Alone in its richest oil regions, exclusive of Emba, exclusive of large recently discovered oil lands, and exclusive of Turkestan, we estimate that the supply available equals 8 billion barrels. The total figure would be even more imposing. On the other hand the riches of all Amer-

[1] *Oil and Gas Journal*, Tulsa, Oklahoma, August 27, 1925.

ica's (U. S. plus Mexico) fields is evaluated at 8 to 9 billion barrels. Finally, Persia and Turkey together have a supply of 5 to 6 billion barrels."

Further, there are the compilations of the United States Geological Survey which supposes that the petroleum reserves of southeast Russia, southwest Siberia and the region of the Caucasus amount to 5,830,000,000 barrels, while those of northern Russia and Sakhalien are estimated at 925,000,000 barrels.[2] In other words, a total of 6,755,000,000 barrels. The same authority credits Persia, Turkey, and Mosul with only 5,820,000,000 barrels, while, according to the recent report of the Federal Oil Conservation Board set up by President Coolidge, the available reserves in the United States amount to no more than 5,500,000,-000 barrels.

As no one will deny the growing importance generally of oil, so no one can gainsay the rôle which the Russian resources are destined to play in world economics and, therefore, in world politics. For the present the Russian oil-fields produce only a small percentage of the total international yield, but the output has increased steadily under Bolshevik management, and, now that American methods have been adopted in the industry and that at least three-fourths of Baku has been electrified, the volume of oil products produced should rise without interruption.

Europe has very limited oil resources outside Russia. The Polish and Roumanian wells are deteriorating, and

---

[2] "Foreign Ownership in the Petroleum Industry"; submitted to U. S. Senate, Washington, 1923.

production in other countries is either very insignificant or still a project. Today the United States supplies its own needs only by importing petroleum from Mexico, and there are indications (which will be discussed in detail later) that the large American oil companies are beginning to fear the loss of their overseas patronage because whatever petroleum may be found in the Western Hemisphere will be required for its own consumption. And it is well within the realm of the possible that before a decade will have elapsed, the United States will be forced to import Russian and Persian "gas."

Merchant marines, navies, railways are adopting oil for fuel purposes more and more. Despite the explorations of engineers in every nook and cranny, in every desert and mountain range of the several continents, an "oil famine" towards the middle of the next decade is not precluded. Within a few years, American oil trusts may be compelled to drop their foreign business as an impossible burden, and the rest of the world will then be dependent for its gasoline, benzine, kerosene, machine oil, etc., on Soviet Russia and Persia, and on Mosul, if any deposits of commercial value are discovered there.

The average citizen may refuse to bother his brains about developments which will come only five or ten years hence. But big business is never so short-sighted, nor is high politics. Men with vision and understanding long ago cast covetous glances towards the oil regions of Russia, towards the rich and delightful Caucasian isthmus in particular, and before the World

War the greater part of the Russian petroleum industry was either directly operated or indirectly controlled by foreign capital, by the Rothschilds, by the Royal Dutch-Shell, by the Nobels, who remained foreigners despite their Russian citizenship, and by others.

The hostilities of 1914–17, and the condition of civil war and chaos which followed immediately upon the Bolshevik revolution offered glorious opportunities to the various Powers to seize the Caucasus (and Sakhalien on the far Pacific) by force of arms. Nor did they shrink from the attempt. Men and money, and in instances even the rational prosecution of the chief objectives of the war, were sacrificed to the thirst for oil. Hans and Fritz, Machmud and Kemal were sent to Gouria and Ganjha and to other places about which they knew little and cared less, for the sake of oil, and long after the world had been made safe for democracy, London Cockneys and Welsh miners were still holding the line in the Caucasus for the British Government and for British petrol associations.

Through the unfortunate accident of losing the war, the Germans and Turks could not retain the Caucasus, and as a result of certain unfortunate flaws in the machinery, British occupation, too, had to end. But this did not mean that the appetite for Russian oil-fields was stilled. On the contrary, it was whetted.

When victory in the World War failed to give the Russian oil prize to any of the Allied nations, they fell to quarrelling for it among themselves. Great Britain, France, Belgium and the United States—these were the factions in the peace-time scramble. One day

England and France stand united against America, the
next France sides with Uncle Sam against Britain, and
then again John Bull and the United States find it
wiser to agree. Subsequently they agree to part ways,
and so the changes continue even unto this very day.
To an extent, the portrayal of the rôle of Soviet oil
in international politics and in the battle royal for
petroleum resources is history. Nevertheless, the
struggle continues. To be sure, the strength of the
Moscow government makes military adventures inex-
pedient, and reduces the likelihood of performances
such as Genoa and The Hague. The facts in the case
are not, therefore, as sensational and spectacular now
as they were in the earlier part of that period which
this volume reviews, but they are not the less interesting
and important for that reason. Indeed, it may be that
a study of the more subtle ways of the giant, world-
wide oil trusts operating often with the secret and
sometimes with the frankly avowed support of their
governments is as absorbing as a recital of the facts of
war-time campaigns, of post-bellum foreign occupation
and of the intrigues at international conferences.

It will be sad to see how the magnet of oil draws
great armies to the Caucasus; it will be fascinating to
examine how the oil companies mobilise the forces of
diplomacy to fight their battles across green tables
and behind the scenes of the Genoa and Hague conferences; it should be enlightening to study how far
the foreign policies of nations, in the matter of recognition, credits, etc., are influenced by that universal
lubricant and irritant—oil, and to what extent the

relations between the two greatest petroleum trusts in the world—the Standard and the Royal Dutch, and between the Standard and Sinclair companies, have been affected by the oil resources of Soviet Russia.

OIL IMPERIALISM

CHAPTER I

THE WAR FOR BAKU

THE real instincts of a man rise to the surface when he is intoxicated; then he acts and speaks the truth. Likewise a nation in time of war. In years of peace, that is, in the intervals between wars, silk-hatted diplomats manœuvre for advantage and position. When open hostilities commence, states don the mailed glove and "grab while the grabbing is good."

In no theatre of the war did we see this better illustrated than in the Near East between 1914 and 1918. In that side-show of the World War where movements on a large scale afforded the Powers wider opportunities of revealing their appetites than did the close, trench warfare in France, the imperialistic aims of Great Britain appeared long before the peace treaties of Versailles and Sèvres gave them legal and honourable sanction. Palestine, Mesopotamia, the Caucasus, North Persia, South Persia—to the English, this broad belt stretching from the Mediterranean to India with the 35th parallel of latitude as its axis meant empire as well as oil. The two can hardly be judged apart.

The Triple Alliance had similar interests in this region. During the first two years of the war German intelligence officers sought to win the Emir of Afghanistan for the cause of the Central Powers. At the same time a German army made itself at home in the neighbouring country of Persia. Here the motive was "empire." But the Berlin-to-Bagdad idea was not merely a piece of Pan-Germanism; it was drenched in oil.[1] The line, as conceived, would have terminated in the Bagdad-Mosul petroleum field. For Germany, therefore, as well as for Great Britain, Mesopotamia (Iraq) conveniently combined empire and oil.

So long as it was possible, the German generals in the World War held to Iraq with might and main. When it was lost, they turned to the Caucasus—for petroleum. And all the time Imperial Turkey strove to extend its territories at the expense of Russia and in the interests of Pan-Islamism—but also of petroleum.

The end of the war drew the curtain on the empire-oil conflict in the Near East and registered a victory for the British. In Palestine and Mesopotamia English endeavour met with permanent success (permanent as far as the word may be used these days); in Persia it was temporarily rewarded. Only in the Russian Caucasus, where the double objective of the Union Jack forces was Baku oil and another lair for the British lion, was Britain thwarted by Bolshevism. On the whole, however, the war to make the world safe for democracy increased Great Britain's petroleum resources many fold,[2] gave her several new colonies, and created buffers for her old possessions.

[1] It was the Anatolian Railway Company, nominally a Turkish concern but actually a German corporation which, as early as 1904, obtained permission from the Porte to explore for oil in Mesopotamia. The company also received an option to develop such resources as it might discover.

[2] The London *Times* of May 7, 1919, reports a speech of Mr. E. G. Prettyman, M.P., a well-known oil authority, at the laying

The scene of these gains was the Near and Middle East. It began very early, this twofold pursuit of precious liquid and precious land.

"The operations of Turkey against Russia," writes L. M. Fanning, of the American Petroleum Institute, "had the Baku oil-fields as their objective, and the early British operations in Mesopotamia (which commenced in 1914) were chiefly intended as a precautionary measure for the protection of the Persian oil-fields." But before long this "precautionary measure" developed into a well-planned advance. While one English army slowly forced its way up from Egypt into Palestine, another marched north into Mesopotamia not, obviously, to guard the oil-fields in Persia, but rather to seize those at Mosul.

To be brief, the British took Bagdad, the capital of Iraq (Mesopotamia) in March, 1917, after a peculiar campaign, the outstanding feature of which was the 147-day Turkish siege of Kut-el-Amara, ending in the capitulation of General Townshend. Upon the fall of Bagdad all the German and Turkish forces in Persia and Mesopotamia were concentrated in the vilayet of Mosul. So important was Iraq in the program of the Central Powers that on April 28, 1917, the Kaiser

of the foundation stone of the new Anglo-Persian refinery, as follows:

"When the war came, the position was, as they all know, that the British Empire with its vast interests in the whole world, controlled about 2 per cent. of the world's petroleum supplies. . . . Now, with the seeds sown and the processes in use, concerning which he had no time to go into detail, he thought that when adjustments were completed the British Empire would not be very far *from controlling one-half of the available* supplies of petroleum in the world." (London *Times*.)

issued a special order instructing von Falkenhayn to retake the country's capital. But the imperial Hohenzollern will notwithstanding, Bagdad remained in British hands.[3]

Though the Turks were now hard pressed by their Tommy enemies in this theatre of the war, we find them transferring great masses of troops to the Russian front. So flagrant was this practice that in June, 1918, Liman von Sanders, the Commander-in-Chief of the Turkish army in Syria, complained to Count Bernstorff, the German ambassador in Constantinople, that "the Turks are sacrificing all Arabia, Palestine and Syria to these boundless undertakings of theirs in the Caucasus." Yet the ambassador calmed the general, for, as we shall see, there was German method in this apparent Turkish madness. Sanders Pasha, anxious to safeguard his own position, and also his own reputation, had one set of interests; the men in Constantinople and Berlin who had a more comprehensive, and therefore more accurate, conception of the entire Eurasian military chessboard, could better judge the comparative importance of Syria and the Russian Caucasus in the general scheme of things. It was they who decided to strengthen the latter front at the expense of the former.

What was happening in Russia in the meantime?

The Czar abdicated his throne in March, 1917, just when the British occupied Bagdad and just when it

---

[3] "And when the armistice was signed the British troops whose line in January, 1918, was not 100 miles beyond Bagdad quickly advanced up the Tigris and occupied Mosul." Davenport and Cooke, *The Oil Trusts and Anglo-American Relations.*

had become possible to create a united British-Russian line six hundred miles long from Trebizond to Erzerum to Bagdad. Thereupon the Slav front broke. The Russian peasants, yearning for peace and anxious to return to productive activity in their villages and fields, bolted and went home. What had been an army effectively barring Turk progress was now—nothing. Thereupon the Sultan's troops entered Russian Armenia.

Kaleidoscopic events were shaking Russia in the meantime. In Petrograd a Provisional Government was formed. But Kerensky and his colleagues dilly-dallied and even proposed to prosecute the war. The régime soon grew endlessly unpopular, and it required but the tiny Bolshevik jolt of November 7, 1917, to destroy its rotten foundations. The Communist Party, led by Lenin and Trotsky, and operating under the slogans of "Peace" and "All Power to the Soviets," now assumed control and commenced broadcasting armistice offers to "All, all, all." A series of tense episodes followed, after which the Bolsheviks were forced to sign without reading the Brest-Litovsk Treaty dictated by the Central Powers. Date, March 3, 1918.

The military collapse of Russia was the signal for a Turk offensive against Kars and Batum, and, subsequently, against Baku. On April 15th the Turks occupied Batum. The strategic gateway of the Caucasus had thus fallen into the hands of the Triple Alliance. Almost simultaneously (April 22nd) the nations of the Caucasus declared themselves autonomous and set up a so-called "Trans-Caucasian Federation" consisting of the Republics of Georgia, Armenia and Azerbaijhan. But though the leaders of these tiny states had solemnly sworn to live together in peace and brotherly love, they soon fell to quarrelling and before a month had passed, democratic Menshevik Georgia, the leading spirit of the "Federation," had declared war on Armenia and Azerbaijhan, the issue in each case being, as Trotsky puts it, "a chip of territory."

Georgia now asked the Germans to give it the pleasure of their presence. Nothing could have fitted in better with German plans. The Triple Alliance had already cast covetous eyes towards Baku—and Georgia is the high-road to Baku. Imagine the joy, then, of Wilhelm II, Hindenburg, Ludendorff, von Tirpitz and the whole Junker clique of reactionary monarchists when the Mensheviks, whose avowed aim it was to establish the socialist heaven on earth, invited them into their beautiful mountain home. Without a moment's hesitation, the German headquarters in the Ukraine and the Crimea sent detachments. On May 25th three thousand German troops under General Kress von Kressenstein landed at the Georgian port of Poti. *On the very same day* the Trans-Caucasian Parliament in Tiflis was dissolved and Noi Jordania, the Menshevik leader, read the Declaration of Independence of the Georgian Menshevik Republic. But this independence assumed very peculiar forms, for on May 28th the Teuton officer von Lossow signed an agreement with Chenkeli, the plenipotentiary of the "independent" republic, by the terms of which the railways and all the naval equipment of Georgia were surrendered to the Germans for the duration of the war. And, subsequently, an agreement was effected giving Turkey the right to carry petroleum free of charge by the Baku-Batum pipe-line. Thereafter, until the Germans left, the Menshevik Republic was merely a puppet and tool in their hands. From Germany came a supplementary division of troops. A German force entered North Persia, occupying Tabriz, and Turks made their first steps into Azerbaijhan, the capital of which is Baku. It was just at this stage that Liman von Sanders protested to Count Bernstorff against the withdrawal of effectives from his Palestinian-Syrian front, but since that day General Ludendorff has been kind enough to explain exactly why so much energy was expended in the Caucasus when the war was about to be decided on the Western front.

"At the Spa conference," writes Ludendorff,[4] "the Imperial Chancellor agreed, with respect to our policy in Georgia, that Colonel von Kress, who had returned to Germany from the Palestine front, was to go to Tiflis as his representative with a guard of one or two companies. It had become necessary that we strengthen our forces there. Altogether apart from our wish for military support from those regions, this was demanded by our supply of raw material. The behaviour of the Turks in Batum had again proven that we could not depend on them in this matter. They had taken all available stores for themselves. We could there-

[4] *Meine Kriegserinnerungen.*

fore expect oil from Baku only if we fetched it ourselves."

The generalissimo proceeds to dilate on the disas-
trous depletion of fuel resources in Germany. The
streets of the cities were dark. The activities of the
German aeroplane squads had been circumscribed in
order to reduce the expenditure of petroleum. Affairs
in this respect were beginning to assume a catastrophic aspect. "The production of oil in Roumania,"
Ludendorff continues, "had as far as possible been
extraordinarily increased. Nevertheless it was out
of the question to think of covering our deficits. This,
however, now seemed possible in Trans-Caucasia, especially in Baku, provided transport facilities would
simultaneously be regulated. . . ." It was accordingly
decided that the "Batum-Tiflis-Baku railway which
had many tank cars on hand was to be put in operation
by Colonel von Kress with the consent of the Turks.
Naturallly the decisive question was how we could get
to Baku." Thus Ludendorff, soldier that he is, bluntly
blurts out the truth.

Plans for the occupation of Baku soon began to
shape themselves. The republic of Azerbaijhan was
persuaded to accept Turkish proffers of aid, and Nuri
Pasha, a half-brother of the famous Enver, marched
into its territory. The Bolsheviks then held control
of Baku. But they were isolated from the rest of
Russia and maintained only imperfect connections with
it by sea. Moreover, considerable internal dissension
had arisen between the Bolsheviks who were unalterably opposed to foreign intervention and the Armenian

Nationalists (Dashnaks) who insisted on inviting the British to Baku. In fact, the Dashnaks had actually sent a delegate to Major-General Dunsterville, in Enzeli, Persia, to invest the city.

The adventures that brought General Dunsterville's "Dunsterforce" to Enzeli are not without interest. They have been told by the gentleman himself.[5] For our purposes the bare outline suffices. He set out from the Bagdad district in February, 1918, with a company of officers. His objective was officially given out to be western Persia, where he was supposedly to prevent an imaginary "German march on India." A few officers were to "prevent" an advance of a German army on India. Such an advance across thousands of miles of roadless and railroadless territory would probably have required hundreds of thousands of men, many months' time and a perfectly organised food, water and reinforcements system. The idea that India can be menaced by an armed force from Russia is preposterous. The Hon. J. M. Balfour, chief assistant to Mr. Armitage-Smith, the British financial adviser of the Persian government in 1920, who is himself an enthusiastic English imperialist, explains in his *Recent Happenings in Persia* that "a very little experience of the difficulties of travel in Persia is sufficient to demonstrate the almost insuperable difficulties which any attempt to move a large scale force across Persia would entail." This is as true of Afghanistan, the only other approach to India. Yet certain British

[5] Major-General Dunsterville, *The Adventures of the Dunsterforce*, 1920.

spokesmen never tire of displaying this bogey to the credulous. The real goal of Dunsterville's mission was Baku, and no less a person than Sir Percy Sykes, commander of the British forces in Persia, contradicts the "India" propagandists by admitting it. He explains that no large force could be sent from Bagdad to Baku, a distance of eight hundred miles.

"The authorities therefore decided to despatch a military mission to reorganise the sound elements of the country into a force that would prevent the Turks and their German masters from reaching Baku. It was hoped that these small states (Georgia, Armenia and Azerbaijhan) would fight for their homes, but the Armenians absolutely failed to do so. Major-General L. C. Dunsterville was appointed to command the mission and, in February, 1918, he started off from Bagdad with a party of officers in forty cars to cross northwest Persia. Enzeli was his objective, and he hoped from that port to be able to proceed to Baku and then to Tiflis." [6]

In other words, no India. The oil of Baku was the objective. It was expected that the natives, "the sound elements," would help the British in reaching it. Dunsterville got to northwest Persia, adopted a White Russian general named Bitcherakov with 1,200 soldiers under his command, subsequently received reinforcements from Bagdad and awaited the opportune moment for the spring across the Caspian to Baku. On August 13th the Bolsheviks decided to evacuate the city. On

[6] Sir Percy Sykes, "Persia," *Encyclopedia Britannica*, Vol. 32.

August 16th Dunsterville with about a thousand men and much artillery appeared on the scene.

Several weeks later, however, great masses of Turkish infantry prepared to close in on the city from all sides. Thereupon Dunsterville calmly took to his ships and returned to Persia without firing a shot (September 13, 1918). The Turks immediately occupied Baku, and immediately (on September 14th) denationalised the oil-fields which a Bolshevik decree of May had declared State property.

The stay of the Turks was short-lived. In November the Armistice between the Allies and Germany was signed. The Turks, in consequence, evacuated Baku and, on November 16th, the British reentered it. They came in boats from Persia, and the flagship, which carried General Thompson, the leader of the expedition, flew the national banners of Great Britain, the United States, France and, be it noted, the flag of the long-deceased Czarist empire. Soon a whole British division was stationed in the Caucasus, and London permitted the troops of none of her allies or associates to share in the pleasure.

The British now proceeded to make themselves at home. They took over the State Bank, the post and telegraph, the courts, etc., and assumed the functions of policing the country and feeding the population. In Georgia they instructed the Menshevik régime as to who of the Communists was to be arrested and who was not to be released. Conveniently enough, the Mensheviks proved as ready to do the bidding of the British general as they had been to obey the dictates of the German colonel only a few months previously.

The English naturally displayed special interest in the Baku oil-fields where their engineers now exercised control.[7] One of the first steps of the British was to establish the British Board of Railway Control at Tiflis, which set to work conditions to the Baku-Batum Railroad on which export oil is carried. Moreover, the Baku-Batum pipe-line was overhauled and its pumping stations repaired.

It must be said in all fairness to the British that their methods in Baku were not depredatory. They did not act as if it were their purpose to seize as much petroleum as possible and escape. They behaved as if they meant to stay for a long, long time. They treated Baku as a new addition to the empire and not as a treasure to be pillaged in passing.[8]

Now the British could well sum up their acquisitions and pride themselves on the attainment. The Caucasus, Persia, Mesopotamia and Palestine lay within their power. It is perhaps fitting that the task of expressing the joy should have fallen to the lot of the

[7] With respect to this British occupation of the Caucasus, Arthur Moore, a well-known British authority of Asia and Islam, writes in the London *Times* of July 10, 1922, as follows:

"After the Armistice we [the British] poured troops into the Caucasus which is largely Musulman. Far across the Caspian we had troops even in the famous Merv. At first these had a stabilizing influence, and we announced that we had come to keep the Bolshevists away. But as soon as the Bolshevist menace began to materialize, it was we who faded away. Why, then, did we go there at all? Islam knows the answer. *We went to try to get hold of the Baku oil-fields, but we were not prepared to fight for them.*" (Italics mine. L. F.)

[8] In 1919, the United Kingdom imported 2,999 tons of oil from Russia; in 1920, the figure rose to 21,680 tons.

chairman of the Bibi Ebat Oil Company, an English combine of several companies which had considerable holdings in Baku. At an annual meeting in London in December, 1918, this practical statesman, Herbert Allen by name, declared: "In the Caucasus from Batum on the Black Sea to Baku on the Caspian, and from Vladikavkaz southward to Tiflis, Asia Minor, Mesopotamia and Persia, British forces have made their appearance and have been welcomed by nearly every race and creed who look to us to free them—some from the Turkish yoke and some from that of Bolshevism."

Then comes this more realistic statement: "Never in the history of these islands was there such an opportunity for the peaceful penetration of British influence and British trade, for the creation of a second India or a second Egypt. . . ."

And finally we have the crux of the situation frankly phrased thus: "The oil industry of Russia liberally financed and properly organised under British auspices would, in itself, be a valuable asset to the empire. . . . A golden opportunity offers itself to the British government to exercise a powerful influence upon the immense production of the Grosni, Baku and Trans-Caspian fields." [9]

Well could England rejoice. The dreams dreamed by British statesmen from Lord Beaconsfield to Lord Curzon were within an inch of realisation. Russia appeared to be crumbling to pieces; it seemed as if Russia had been eliminated as a factor in the Near

[9] London *Financial News,* December 24, 1918.

East. The empire had gained territory and oil, and lost a traditional enemy.

England's policy has always been the dismemberment of Russia. It was for this reason that it supplied with arms, ammunition, officers, money and advice such counter-revolutionary leaders as Denikin and Koltchak. Boris Savinkov, who was Denikin's agent in Paris and London, and in that capacity conferred with Churchill, Lloyd George and others, testified at his trial in Moscow in August, 1924, that "the English, for example, told me often and insistently that it would be desirable to establish an independent Southeastern Union consisting of North Caucasus and Trans-Caucasia, and said that this Union would be only a beginning, that later Azerbaijhan and Georgia would have to join it. In all this I sensed the odor of petroleum."

Britain wished to divide and then be the patron and protector of the parts. This explains why Denikin, whose base was southeastern Russia, received support from the English. And because they supported Denikin they felt that they could themselves evacuate for the time being. In August, 1919, the British army of occupation left the Caucasus, not, however, before the British naval squadron on the Caspian, which had been reequipped with modern, powerful guns, had been moved secretly—so as not to arouse the Azerbaijhan nationalists—from Baku to Derbent, where it was transferred to Denikin. A garrison remained to keep open the door, the port of Batum.

Chicherin, the Soviet Commissar for Foreign Affairs, thus explains the action of the British:

"On the one hand, this [the evacuation] was brought about by the mood of the British masses and of the British army which made it impossible for England to continue the struggle with English troops, and Anglo-Indian forces were too weak—on the other hand, England at the moment was so certain that her enemy [Russia] was buried, and that no other enemy could be expected, that with a light heart she threw the Caucasus to her agents, the reactionary Caucasian governments.[10]

"In 1919," Chicherin stated on the same occasion, "England was so certain that we [the Bolsheviks] could never advance as far as the Caucasus that Lloyd George at the Lord Mayor's banquet in the autumn stated it as an axiom that in Russia a rift was taking place between South Russia and Central Russia; that South Russia could under no circumstances subdue Central Russia nor could Central Russia possibly conquer South Russia;[11] that for England this was very

[10] In January, 1920, the Allied Supreme Council recognised the Republics of Georgia and Azerbaijhan. In February, Admiral McCully, the United States representative at the headquarters of General Denikin, informed Denikin that his government could not subscribe to the decision of the Supreme Council to recognise the republics of Georgia and Azerbaijhan. Hereupon Denikin expressed his thanks. (Hague *Newve Courant*, February 16, 1920, and Berlin *Deutsche Allgemeine Zeitung*, February 23, 1920.) The American attitude is easily explained by the fear of the Standard Oil that the two little British vassals in the Caucasus would close the door to the Rockefeller firm, which already had heavy interests in Baku, and grant a monopoly to its world rivals, the Royal Dutch-Shell and Anglo-Persian companies. By refusing to recognise Georgia and Azerbaijhan America left the door open to a protest against any disposition they would make of Caucasian petroleum. The refusal was likewise consonant with the then attitude of the United States in favor of an undivided Russia.

[11] Chicherin here refers to Lloyd George's speech on November

fine because it signified the weakening of that great foe with which Great Britain had always struggled and the fulfillment of what Beaconsfield had always dreamt."

The retention of a military nucleus at Batum was significant. It meant that Britain intended some day to return. At the Peace Conference in Paris English statesmen suggested the setting up of Batum as a free state under the ægis of the League of Nations, and only when the Supreme Council finally abandoned this idea which had previously been incorporated in a draft of the Treaty of Sèvres did the Tommy garrison leave Batum (July 7, 1920). The city was then transferred to the Menshevik republic of Georgia, over which Great Britain continued to maintain a paternal watch.

English interest in Georgia is not accidental. Limitless confidence in the success of Denikin, plus the embarrassing opposition to further military occupation in Russia on the part of the British labor movement had finally brought about the evacuation of the Caucasus, but Menshevik Georgia still opened a door of hope.

Through Georgia passes the Batum-Baku pipe-line. Georgia is the key to the Caucasus and controls the

10, 1919, in the Guildhall, in which, after describing the alternate advances and retreats of the rival armies in Russia, he said: "Therefore, you must not imagine that I am reading from the present situation any sort of prediction that the Bolshevists are going to conquer the whole of Russia. I do not believe it. [Cheers.] The free peasantry of the South have in their hearts a detestation of Bolshevism, and I do not believe that the Bolshevists will ever conquer that aversion."

road from Europe to Baku. Baku oil designated for export purposes must have transit through Georgia. As long as the Mensheviks remained in control at Tiflis, the chances of the British were not yet dead.[12] But in April, 1920, Bolsheviks entered Baku and in February, 1921, Georgia turned Bolshevik.

This was the end of a seven years' struggle on the part of Turkey, Germany and England to acquire the Caucasus, and Baku in particular. There can be no doubting the decisive rôle played by Baku in this important chapter of the World War. "Had there been no oil at Baku," writes W. J. Childs, formerly of the Intelligence Department of the British Admiralty and a recognised expert on eastern affairs, "events in the

---

[12] Several attempts have been made to reestablish Menshevism in Georgia. With regard to the last uprising, in August, 1924, Dr. Nonnebruch, a well-known German authority, writes in the *Deutsche Zeitung,* an outspokenly reactionary and anti-Bolshevik Berlin daily, as follows (September 17, 1924): "And just at the time when the British oil statesmen realised that the Anglo-Russian trade agreement would bring no results in the realm of oil politics, the [Menshevik] insurrection in South Russia [Caucasus] was raised. . . . And Jordania, the president of the [Menshevik] Georgian federal government [of 1918–20] suggests international arbitration which would, in effect, be a diplomatic covering for the oil companies."

That the oil companies have a special interest in the detachment of Georgia from Soviet Russia by means of a Menshevik revolt also appears from an article in Paris *Le Courrier des Petroles,* September 12, 1924: "At any rate we may inquire whether they [the Georgian Mensheviks] really expected to depend only upon their own resources. The conditions under which the revolt broke out, as well as the way in which the large European metropoles were rapidly and properly informed of its progress, permit the thought that the revolutionary movement has received serious material support. It also probably approximates the truth to say that this support comes from groups which defend large petroleum interests. . . .

"It should, furthermore, be noted that this attempt represents the last card of the former owners in Russia, expropriated

Near and Middle East during the years 1913–1921 would have shown a striking dissimilarity from the events which actually befell." The facts confirm his opinion. For Baku is not merely a "finger extended towards Asia," as Chicherin, with an eye to the city's geographical shape, so aptly described it, but also probably the earth's largest single oil-field. Moreover, the master of Baku is likely to gain control of Grosni as well.

No military expense was spared in the endeavour to win the Caucasus. The Turkish campaigns against the Caucasus, for instance, cost the Sultan more men than any other Ottoman activity during the war. Germany went far from her base and weakened herself on other fronts to occupy this region which, from the

by the revolution. If they fail in this desperate move, there can be no doubt that the Soviets will regard the confiscation as definite and final. . . ."

Subsequent to the last Menshevik insurrection the present author visited Georgia and spent six weeks in the Caucasus. The following excerpt is from his article on the revolt which was printed in *The Nation* (New York) of December 17, 1924: "Before me," it reads, "is a letter written by Noi Jordania, president of Menshevik Georgia, and intercepted by the Cheka. He outlines his plans to his comrades. First Daghestan is to revolt. Then Azerbaijhan and the Mountain Republic centering around Vladikavkaz. Finally Georgia. With the Caucasus thus detached from Russia they could prepare the downfall of Bolshevism." This is the "oil state" of which French papers wrote and which, it was suggested, would be under the aegis of the League.

Finally, there is the evidence of *The New York Times* to prove that oil interests are involved in what is generally represented as the struggle for the independence of Georgia. On September 13, 1924, the paper printed a dispatch from its Paris correspondent which stated that: "It is understood, according to well-informed persons, that the revolution is being financed and directed from Paris, where powerful international financiers are backing a group of former members of the Georgian [Menshevik] government and former proprietors of Baku oil wells."

strategic point of view, was for her, and at that time at least, a greater liability than an asset. The reason, as Ludendorff unequivocally testifies, was oil. And England seized the first opportunity to drive towards Baku.

The less violent methods which the Powers subsequently adopted in their efforts to acquire the oil of the Caucasus should therefore be no cause for surprise.

CHAPTER II

THE GENOA CONFERENCE AND OIL

GENOA was the first wholesale attempt of the big oil trusts, acting with the support of their respective Foreign Offices, to establish themselves in the Caucasus by peaceful means. The Conference was convened to hasten the course of Europe's post-bellum economic rehabilitation, and while the Russian problem soon eclipsed every other and in the end caused the break-up of the conference, neither the question of, nor even the term, Russian oil, was ever mentioned at any of its plenary sessions or in any of the notes and memoranda exchanged by the several delegations. The protocols of the assembly will show as little reference to petroleum as to helium gas; officially, neither Lloyd George, nor Barthou for France, nor Chicherin, Litvinov, Krassin or Rakovsky for Russia, nor Schanzer or Facta for Italy, nor Rathenau or Wirth for Germany, nor Benes or Theunis or Skirmundt or any of the world's greatest statesmen who gathered at Genoa ever gave a thought during the six weeks of the conference to so sordid a subject as petroleum. Nevertheless it will not be difficult to prove that oil occupied the centre of the Genoa stage, and that through it one can find the key to more of the misunderstandings and crises of the conference than through any of the questions which actually formed the basis of open discussion.

Soviet petroleum concessions played a very decisive rôle in the Genoa conference deliberations. And it will be seen that the United States, which was represented by an "observer" only part of the time, was an important, perhaps the most important, participant in the struggle for oil which went on behind the scenes of the conference, ultimately torpedoing it.

Months before the diplomats assembled in the ancient Italian seaport, the Standard Oil Company and the Anglo-Persian Oil Company had entered into an agreement with regard to the north Persian, Palestinian and Mesopotamian petroleum fields. But the Standard Oil had arrived at no arrangement with the Royal Dutch-Shell group as to the Caucasus. Both these companies held very heavy interests in the Caucasus, and the one was intent on preventing the other from anticipating it in that rich petroleum region. A. C. Bedford, Chairman of the Board of Directors of the Standard Oil, stated the position of his company very clearly in an interview which he gave the London *Times* on April 12th, two days after the opening of the Genoa Conference.

"We feel," he said, "that there should be no attempt at the Genoa Conference, or through private agreement among various nations, to exploit the resources of Russia; but that it should be understood that a fair and equal economic opportunity should be preserved for all concerned."

Now, oil men, especially taciturn Standard Oil men of the Bedford type, do not grant interviews merely to help newspaper correspondents. Among the "all concerned" his own firm was uppermost, at least for him, and his statement was a broad hint to the others concerned, the Royal Dutch-Shell in particular, that the Standard Oil was bent on having a "fair and equal opportunity" when it came to dividing the resources of Baku. It is obvious, too, that Mr. Bedford expected the matter to be discussed, either officially or unofficially, at the conference. Finally, Bedford's words permitted the *Times* reader to suppose that some negotiations with a view to exploiting Russia's petroleum resources had already taken place, and that the Standard director feared lest an agreement on this matter might really be signed at Genoa, where his competitors could have easy access to the big Bolshevik chiefs.

There had, indeed, been negotiations between the Royal Dutch-Shell and Krassin, the Red envoy in London,[1] and at the very moment when Mr. Bedford used the columns of the friendly Northcliffe press to issue his warning against any infringement of his company's interests in Russia, Colonel Boyle, a romantic figure, was in the Caucasus on behalf of the Royal Dutch-Shell. Boyle had for some time past been conducting negotiations with Krassin in London and had now gone to South Russia to investigate the Shell's former properties. He had originally approached Mr. Krassin with a letter of introduction from none other than Lord Curzon, who, it will be recalled, asserted at Lausanne that he had never spoken to an oil man in his

[1] The Shell had even prepared the draft of a concession contract.

life. Curzon caused his Under-Secretary to write as follows:

FOREIGN OFFICE,
19TH OCTOBER 1921,

MONSIEUR KRASSIN.

SIR,

The Marquis Curzon of Kedleston is informed by Colonel J. W. Boyle that the Royal Dutch-Shell group are anxious to obtain a concession from the Soviet Government for the production of oil from their properties in South Russia and Caucasia.

I am directed to inform you that it is with the full approval and support of His Majesty's Government that Colonel Boyle has addressed himself to you on this subject. His Majesty's Government trusts that these negotiations may result in an early and satisfactory settlement.

I am,
Sir,
Your most obedient servant,

(Signed)   ESMOND OVEY.

Several days later Krassin's secretary replied that "Lieutenant Colonel J. W. Boyle has been given an opportunity of explaining to Mr. Krassin the views and desires of the Naphtha interests represented by him in connection with concessions for the exploitation of the oil wells formerly owned by them in South Russia and Caucasus."

We must note, in the first place, that the efforts of the Royal Dutch-Shell to obtain a Russian petroleum concession had the blessing and assistance of the British government, and, furthermore, that whereas

Lord Curzon wrote of "their properties in South Russia and Caucasus," Krassin's answer referred to "oil wells *formerly* owned by them." This difference was a cardinal point.

The properties of the Royal Dutch-Shell made it the largest former owner of oil-fields in Russia. Its first interests were acquired in 1912 when the Shell purchased 80 per cent. of the Rothschild Frères holdings in Baku in consideration of 241,227 pounds sterling of shares in the English Shell Company and 3,879,000 guldens of stock in the Dutch Koninklijke Company. Shortly afterwards additional 10 per cent. were bought from the French firm, and soon the Rothschild house became a mere bank representative of the Royal Dutch-Shell in Paris.

After the revolution, Sir Henri Deterding, the president of the Royal Dutch, of whom Admiral Lord Fisher had said, he is "Napoleonic in boldness and Cromwellian in depth," conceived the idea of becoming the sole master of the great oil wealth of the Caucasus. With this object in view, and speculating on the fall of the Soviets or on their ultimate recognition of private property rights, the whale commenced swallowing as many of the small fish as possible. Minor companies were bought outright, and in July, 1920, the Bataafische Petroleum Company, one of the richest subsidiaries of Mr. Deterding's corporation, purchased large blocks of shares in the two largest independent Russian oil concerns; Mantashev and Lianosov. About the same time the Shell acquired the Nikopol-Mariupol Pipe Factory, the largest pipe factory in Russia, for

£250,000. Deterding wished, by owning it, to round out his possessions in the Caucasus, for the works put him in a position to lay as many oil pipe-lines as were required.

The only important competitor of the Royal Dutch in Caucasian oil claims was now the Standard Oil Company. Even before the war it had been rumored that the House of Rockefeller had interests in Nobel & Company, which then controlled approximately 40 per cent. of the production of Baku. While the Genoa Conference was in session the Standard issued the following statement:

"Immediately after the war, negotiations were begun between representatives of the Nobel Company and the Standard Oil Company of New Jersey looking to a sale to the latter of participation in the Nobel properties. Early in the summer of 1920 the sale was consummated and the Nobel and Standard Oil became equal partners in the Nobel's Russian oil properties. There has been no change in the situation since that time." [2]

The Genoa stage was thus set for a struggle between the two world oil giants: the Standard and the Royal Dutch-Shell. There were also other companies. In fact, before Genoa one hundred and sixty tiny as well as titanic petroleum companies supporting claims to properties in Baku, Grosni, Emba, Maikop, etc., had been listed. Now when the Bolsheviks took possession of the Caucasus, they nationalised all these properties, thereby annulling the claims which any private owner

[2] Paris *New York Herald*, May 13, 1922.

might make upon them. The private owners, however, branded the nationalisation act of the Soviets as illegal and continued to regard certain plots of ground and certain wells in the Caucasus as their own. Stocks of various Caucasian oil companies were quoted on the Bourse and were looked upon as desirable objects of exchange.

In the meantime, the Bolsheviks proceeded with the exploitation of the oil-fields, and in 1921, the first year of the Russian peace, produced 246,400,000 poods (4,100,000 tons), which represented 43.9 per cent. of the 1913 norm. But production was expensive, domestic consumption of oil greatly reduced, export in large quantities impossible on account of a crippled transport system and the competition of antagonistic trusts, and capital for improvements and development almost entirely lacking. Moreover, the Bolsheviks must have believed, somewhat erroneously as subsequent events proved, that their government could obtain no recognition, their industries no credits and their banks no loans, as long as the mighty in the oil world were not appeased by concessions.

This was the real situation at the dawn of Genoa. The Soviet delegation arrived at the conference with a prepared scheme for oil concessions. As Krassin stated in Genoa to a correspondent of the Paris *L'Informa-tion*, the Russian government wanted to give a place to each of the Great Powers—France, England, Germany, Italy, Belgium, and even the United States—on condition that a part of the oil-fields was reserved to Russia. The area of oil land which were subject to foreign concessions, Krassin continued, would not be greater than 3,000 hectares (approximately 7,500 acres), which would mean an area of between 200 and 1,000 hectares for each of the Powers.[3]

Genoa now became a magnet for the petroleum men of the earth. The conference, so the dailies wrote, was to be the field on which the battle for Russian oil would be fought. And actually, oil kings, great and small, did commence to flock to the Italian city. They came as "observers." But the real purpose of each was to extract something from the Red delegation, and failing that, to play the part of the dog in the manger. With some writers, the rôle of oil in Genoa was not an afterthought. They saw it as an inevitable development. Thus we find the Manchester *Guardian Commercial*, writing on April 13th, that "with Russia represented at the Genoa conference, one of the most important points for discussion is oil," while as early as April 6th —four days before the conference opened,—the Paris correspondent of the *Rheinisch Westfälische Zeitung*, the organ of the heavy industrialists of the Ruhr, wired: "There are people who believe that the history of the Genoa Conference will be written in oil. The conference will really be the scene of the struggles between the Standard Oil and the Royal Dutch companies."

The people who so believed were probably not few, for the joust between these two world oil giants had already cast its shadow before, and realists were prepared for an interesting fray.

The official proceedings of the Genoa Conference

[3] London *Times*, May 2, 1922.

began on April 10, 1922. On April 13th, Wickham
Steed, the editor of the London *Times*, was already
wiring his paper that "Genoa has become a stage for
the Bolshevists," and three days later he recorded his
distress over the circumstance that "they [the Bolshe-
viks] are the arbiters of the conference." From the
very beginning the chief point of interest was the debts
of the Czarist and Kerensky régimes to foreign creditors, and the private property of non-Russians which
the Bolsheviks had confiscated. Several days after the
conference opened a semi-official discussion on this subject took place between Lloyd George, Barthou and
the Soviet delegation. "M. Litvinov having maintained
the impossibility of restoring private property to its
former owners, either Russian or foreign, Mr. Lloyd
George suggested that a way out might be found by
restoring it on principle on a *99 years' lease*." [4] On
this occasion it was announced that the Allies' claim
on Russia amounted to 2,600,000,000 British pounds.
Whereupon Litvinov presented Russia's counter-claim
of 5,000,000,000 British pounds for damage done by
the troops of the Allies and their Russian friends during the 1918–20 period of Civil War and military intervention.

It was around this question that the open and officially chronicled dispute of the conference centred.
The Bolsheviks refused to denationalise the property
they had appropriated, or to recognise any private
claims upon it, much less to restitute it. Before this
world tribunal at which all the Powers were gathered

[4] London *Times*, April 16, 1922.

they publicly flouted the sacred rights of private property. France and Belgium were incensed. But from the very outset Lloyd George adopted a very friendly and conciliatory attitude towards the Muscovites; so friendly and conciliatory that it could not but have aroused suspicion.

The Franco-Belgian reluctance to concede the leasehold principle as advocated by Lloyd George was the direct cause of the rift in the Allied front which prevented any agreement with the Bolsheviks.

"There appears to be some difference of opinion," reads Wickham Steed's wire from Genoa dated April 28th, "between the British delegation on the one hand and the Belgian delegation on the other as to the length to which the Allies can go in the hope of finding a basis of agreement with the Bolshevists. The British view seems to be that the Allies can accept the Bolshevist principle of nationalisation provided that private properties which have been seized be returned to their owners on a 99 years' lease. The Belgian view is, on the contrary, that the maintenance of the freehold principle is essential in order to insure the rights of private property in Russia and so as not to give a handle to the Communist parties of European states, which might invoke the Bolshevist precedent and demand that all owners of private property be declared to be holding it only on a 99 years' lease."

For days and days the discussion on this question of private property continued. Not a word of oil was there either in the newspapers or at the sessions. All discussion was concentrated on "debts," "credits," "confiscation," "restitution," etc. The relations between the British and French delegations were steadily growing colder, the friction steadily greater. Even the crafty Lloyd George could, apparently, find no formula to bridge the divergence between the British and Franco-Belgian views, a divergence which, after all, was only academic. For there was practically as much difference between a 99 years' lease and freehold ownership under the Soviets as there is between six and half a dozen. If the former owners felt that a century agreement was insufficient protection because the Bolsheviks might any day arbitrarily annul it, then they surely realised that just as little faith could be put in Bolshevik restitution of their property. The Russians could any day arbitrarily annul the restitution too. It is obvious that so sharp a break as ultimately developed between the British and the French and Belgians was not to be explained by this comparatively small variation in their views. The cause was deeper.

Meanwhile the Germans had thrown their well-known bomb into the conference by signing the Rapallo Treaty with the Russians.[5] By its terms Germany recognised the Soviet state de jure, and both nations renounced all claims which they had upon one another. The French and the Belgians flew into a holy rage. Lloyd George and the Italians went through the motions of doing likewise, for the Germans had made the step so clumsily, and at so unpropitious a time, that much public opinion was easily aroused against the Berlin delegates. But

[5] The treaty was signed on April 16th and published on April 18th.

Lloyd George had been kept privately informed of the progress of the Russo-German negotiations which led to the treaty during their entire course. Members of the British delegation were kept au courant by Rathenau and Wirth. Rathenau issued a statement to this effect when the storm over the Rapallo agreement first broke. To save his skin Lloyd George denied the fact. *He* had not known of the *treaty*. But his subordinates in the delegation had known of the negotiations which led to it. Subsequent to Lloyd George's dementi, Rathenau reaffirmed his statement. What with the avalanche of protests that almost drowned the Germans in those days, and what with their very defensive attitude, he would never have dared to throw out such a challenge if he had not been telling the truth. The British were not opposed to a Russo-German understanding in 1922 though to mollify their Allies they feigned being so. But the French and Belgians were violent. They demanded the exclusion of the Germans from the conference, and sought to make the incident an excuse for the disruption of the gathering. Why?

On May 11th the Berlin *Lokal Anzeiger*, a reactionary, monarchist paper which could not be suspected of an atom of sympathy for Soviet Russia, offered the following explanation:

"It is they [the Standard Oil interests] which have stiffened the opposition of the French and the Belgians to the Rapallo Treaty. Not that these interests are opposed to any exploitation in Russia, but they consider the present moment of financial stringency of the Soviet government as sufficiently favourable to enable them finally to arrive at some co-ownership of Russian petroleum deposits, the richest in the world after the American. Without this support from America, France, which furnishes the Prætorian guard for this trust, would hardly oppose Great Britain in this manner." [6]

We shall see that this was indeed the line-up: France and Belgium supported by the Standard Oil and supporting the Standard Oil's view that either that company is permitted to take possession of the property to which its deal with Nobel would ordinarily have entitled it, or all firms refrain from entering into relations with the Soviet government; on the other hand, the British government supporting the Royal Dutch-Shell's efforts to obtain a large concession from the Bolsheviks, Italy indifferently seconding England, and Germany rather neutral.

All these weeks the Allies at the conference were busy trying to draft an ultimatum to the Russians on the question of private property. But no agreement could be attained. Neither would Lloyd George make any concession to the Franco-Belgian principle, nor would the Franco-Belgian bloc yield to the British.

Presently rumours of an all-inclusive petroleum concession to the Royal Dutch-Shell in the Caucasus commenced to circulate. Henry Rollin, the correspondent in Genoa of the *Temps*, wired his paper a long and

---

[6] On April 26th, Chicherin, in an interview with the Genoa correspondent of the Paris *Temps*, stated that the real reason for the change to harshness of the tone of the Allies was their desire to put pressure on Russia and Germany to force Russia to abandon her point of view in regard to private property.

sensational story in which he definitely affirmed that the concession to Shell had already been signed. Excitement knew no bounds. Denials and declarations flashed through air. On May 2nd the Reuter Agency carried this telegram from Genoa: "The Russian delegation flatly denies that any concession has been made to the Shell Oil and the Royal Dutch Companies, though M. Krassin today admitted that the Shell, the Royal Dutch and the Anglo-Persian Companies have been negotiating with the Soviet authorities on the subject. The latter, however, are opposed in principle to any kind of concession and would certainly not agree to one of a general character. They might, however, agree to a local concession but would grant even that only when the Soviet Government had been recognised. M. Krassin added that the Standard Oil Company had made no offers."

The same day inquiries at Shell House in London proved vain . . . "neither confirmation nor denial could be obtained of the report from Genoa" [7] concerning the rumoured oil concession. On that very day, too, Colonel Boyle, the Royal Dutch-Shell representative who had arrived in Genoa from the Caucasus, announced through Reuter that "he had been negotiating with M. Krassin for several months in regard to oil concessions under the trade agreement between Great Britain and the Soviet Government. He had seen M. Krassin since his arrival, and had informed him that he could not talk business of any sort until the conclusion of the Genoa conference and until the rela-

[7] London *Times*, May 3, 1922.

tions between the governments concerned had been defined. That is the real position, and the statement that there had been an agreement with the Soviet Government was absolutely false."

No agreement had been signed. Yet between the words of Krassin's and Colonel Boyle's affirmations one could see that a concession was under discussion, that perhaps an agreement was all but concluded. At any rate the diplomats in the enemy camp put no trust and found no comfort in the statement either of the Soviet delegate or of the British oil man. On the day they were made, Barthou, the head of the French delegation, left Genoa for Paris to consult Poincaré on the situation which had arisen.

Now all attention is concentrated on oil. The memorandum which the conference has sent to the Soviet delegates on the subject of private property is practically forgotten. There are no plenary sessions and a lull prevails over all the deliberations of the sub-commissions of the conference. The press feels the pulse of the situation and mirrors its tenseness.

"The press is full of oil today," wires the Paris correspondent of the London *Times* on May 7th. "Movements of oil magnates and alleged draft agreements to sign which the Bolsheviks are only awaiting the end of the conference. While it is impossible to exaggerate the importance which oil may have in a future Russian settlement, it is clear that, having regard to the great conflicting interests involved and the difficulty of checking statements presumably made with the object of promoting or countering the aims of various actual or potential concessionaires, views on this subject need to be accepted with the utmost caution. What is certain is that the French have at last awakened to the desirability of being specially represented at Genoa in the matter of oil, and M. Laurent-Eynac, Under-Secretary of State for Aeronautics [8] has gone there to keep an eye on the proceedings of foreign oil negotiations."

It should be borne in mind that there were no French companies with large holdings in the Caucasus, or in any other Russian oil-field, before the revolution. According to an article by Dr. W. Mautner in the Vienna-Berlin *Petroleum* quoted with approval by the London *Petroleum Times* of March 28, 1925, "French interests in the Russian oil-fields, as represented by a few important companies, amount to 67,785,000 gold roubles" ($34,000,000). One does not wreck so great a conference for so small a sum. The Belgian investment in the Russian oil industry, after the same authority, was even more minute and amounted in all to $21,000,000, while that of the British exceeded those of France and Belgium combined—171,424,300 roubles ($85,712,150) to be exact.[9]

Why then did France require special representation

---

[8] On April 20, 1920, M. Laurent-Eynac had been appointed Chief Commissar for Petroleum Affairs. Four days later the San Remo oil agreement was signed.

[9] The official pre-war Russian record, compiled by P. V. Ohl, of the Institute of Economic Research of the Commissariat of Finance, in his *Foreign Capital in Russia* (Petrograd, 1922), cites even smaller figures for French and Belgian capital in the Russian oil industry. It gives the French participation as 51,115,000 roubles, the Belgian as 6,812,500 roubles and the British as 171,400,000 roubles.

in the matter of oil? Obviously M. Laurent-Eynac's mission was not so much to look after minor pre-revolutionary French interests as to reconnoitre on behalf of a powerful corporation which laid claim to 40 per cent. of Baku.

The news-hounds in Genoa were now let loose on the scent of oil. The conference had dissolved itself into a chase for the precious liquid, and the journalists on the scene struggled hard to understand the course which events were taking. Why was the conference at a standstill? Was the main official concern of the conference—the problem of the restitution of private property in Russia—a mere smoke-screen for the oil men of contending countries operating behind the backs of their respective diplomats? Had or had not a concession been granted? What was the position of Standard Oil? Would the American government interfere? etc., etc. Such were the intriguing mysteries.

The correspondent of the *News of the World* of London came nearest to a solution. The *News of the World*, a journal of the divorce-case, murder-trial type, is not one which would usually be quoted in such a connection, but special circumstances justify it here. The paper is owned by Lord Riddell, a close personal friend of Lloyd George. Lord Riddell was himself in Genoa and there is reason to believe that the newspaper's representative in the conference city received his inspiration, if not all his information, directly from the British delegation, perhaps even from its chief. "The Standard Oil Company," reads his despatch of May 6th, "one of the greatest secret forces of the world, is now fighting to prevent a Russian settlement on lines which they believe would give British oil interests virtual control of the great Russian oil industry."

The Standard Oil had ample reason for believing that a settlement would have given the Royal Dutch-Shell "virtual control" of Caucasian oil. In the first place, it was generally known that Sir Henri Deterding had ambitions in this direction. He wished to buy all of Baku, and probably all of Grosni. But it was not until the "Allied" memorandum of May 2nd was penned and forwarded to the Russians that the storm broke. Why? Because had a settlement been arrived at on the basis of that document, the Standard Oil's claim in the Caucasus would have been invalidated.

Around the memorandum of May 2nd the entire tempest of the conference centred. The issue was the nature of the concession to be granted. The Bolsheviks had originally contemplated an amalgamation of all the oil interests into one mixed company in which the Soviet government too would participate. In fact, Krassin, who was in charge of the Russian oil negotiations at Genoa, actually outlined such a concession to a representative of the *Matin*.[10] The Moscow government, Krassin stated, proposed retaining one-quarter of Baku for itself. The rest it would divide into three or four sections. One would be given to the British, another to the Americans, another to the French, Belgians, etc. Provision would also be made for a settle-

[10] Quoted by the Moscow *Isvestia,* May 9, 1922.

ment with the former Russian owners who might likewise, in one form or another, become members of the
"consortium". The whole operation, however, Krassin
insisted, would have to be under single technical
management.

Such an arrangement was unsatisfactory to the
Royal Dutch-Shell. It would have given the Standard
Oil, its chief rival, privileges similar to its own. Moreover, it would have wiped out any advantage which
the Deterding-Samuel organisation had won through
its London negotiations with Krassin prior to the
conference. Accordingly, the British delegation at
Genoa exerted every effort to clear the way to a
monopoly concession, or at least to a concession in
which the English company would secure a predominant position. It succeeded in the memorandum of
May 2nd

The mooted clause of this historic paper was Article
VII. One of the paragraphs pledged the Soviet
government not to "hand over to other parties" properties which could not be returned to their former
owners. This, obviously, would have prevented the
granting to one company of an entire field, since each
field had been held by many owners. But the paragraph immediately following it solved the difficulty by
annulling it.

"If the exploitation of the property," it reads,
"can only be executed by its merger into a larger group
the preceding provision shall not apply, but the previous owner shall be entitled to participate in the
group in proportion to his former rights."

Now the road was open to a merger-concession, but room was still left for the participation of the Standard Oil and all the other Shell competitors. The British, therefore, injected yet a third paragraph which defined a former owner as an individual or group of individuals who had held property in Russia *before the nationalisation act of the Bolsheviks*. Now the Standard Oil had purchased its holdings in Baku from Nobel in 1920. That was two years *after* the nationalisation act of the Bolsheviks. This third paragraph, in other words, effectually barred the Standard Oil from the merger-concession. It also barred most of the French interests which consisted of paper bought on the Paris Bourse since 1918. Small wonder, then, that Poincaré instructed Barthou not to sign this "Allied" memorandum. Nor did the Belgians sign.

The "merger", if it had been formed under the provisions of Article VII, would have been dominated by the Anglo-Dutch trust. Some French and Belgian companies, and a few minor British firms such as the Spies Petroleum and the Baku Consolidated, might have entered into the combine, but they would have been overawed and crushed by the financial strength of the Shell.

The Standard Oil cannot be censured for opposing such a settlement with all the means in its power even to the extent of American government intervention. It stood in danger of losing a claim to property worth tens of millions of dollars, and its arch-enemy, the Royal Dutch, enjoyed the prospect of obtaining a monopoly over Baku, than which there is no richer field in the world, with perhaps Grosni added in the bargain. The Rockefeller directors were fighting for what they considered their just rights.

Nor can the British be blamed. The Russians, it is true, had prepared a scheme for an international, all-inclusive concession in which all countries were to have had equitable participation, this on the assumption that old claims would be erased and forgotten. But when the capitalists commenced demanding either compensation or restitution as a *sine qua non,* the Russian scheme became unfeasible. The former owners demanded the return of their properties in the one case; compensation proportionate to their holdings in the second. This being so, a fair division to the oil companies of the several Powers irrespective of by-gones was out of the question. It then became a matter of which claims the Soviets recognised and which they did not. They did not recognise claims acquired after nationalisation. That is immutable Communist principle. The Bolsheviks tell you that they cannot be expected to honour a claim based on a private transaction in which one party transfers to another property which both know the State has declared its own. The Nobel-Standard Oil was just such a transaction. The Standard knew that Nobel's holdings had been declared nationalised. Nevertheless it bought them. That was its loss, the Russians argue. With such claimants they were not prepared to negotiate on compensation. Now if the British had insisted on Soviet recognition of post-1918 claims, a settlement would have been impossible. Accordingly, they framed

Article VII of the May 2nd memorandum so as to make it more acceptable to the Bolsheviks. It should be remembered, however, that they did so gladly, for its terms excluded a dangerous rival—the Standard Oil Company.

We return now to the message sent from Genoa to Lord Riddell's weekly journal. After dilating on the importance of Russian oil, and the history of the industry since nationalisation, he comes to speak of the negotiations between the Shell and the Bolsheviks.

"As soon as the Cannes conference decided upon the meeting at Genoa," the despatch then continues, "all negotiations were suspended, as the Shell people wanted to know the effect of the conference and take advantage of any general settlement reached concerning private property.

"These negotiations have not been resumed, and there are absolutely no contracts, and no agreement has been signed. Such is the position in a nutshell and it disposes of all rumours to the contrary, however circumstantial. Colonel Boyle refuses to make known the tenor of his negotiations with Krassin, but the Russian circles do not deny the story put out by the American oil interests that the Soviets are about to give the Royal Dutch-Shell a lease on some of the communal oil districts subject to a royalty, and to appoint a Shell distribution agent abroad for oil belonging to the Soviet government. Representatives of the Standard Oil Company have been in Genoa for weeks, but have been unable to get anything out of the Soviets. Then came the reports . . . that the Shell had obtained important concessions. Despite the denials of Colonel Boyle and Hon. W. Samuel, chairman of the Shell Company, the story [of the concession] greatly increased the atmosphere of suspicion at Genoa."

And now we arrive at some very sensational revelations which subsequent events proved to be true. "It is believed," continues the despatch, "that before the publication of the story [of the Shell concession] American oil interests had been active in Belgium and Paris, warning the governments concerned against so-called British greed. Belgium's demand for the return of private property without leaving Russia the option of compensation, and the French amendment to the Russian memorandum may both have been thus influenced. It is also known that American oil interests brought pressure to bear at Washington to obtain a declaration from the American government in favor of an open-door policy in Russia." This declaration was soon to be made.

There is a frank hint here that the Franco-Belgian opposition had previously been whipped up by the Standard Oil. Numerous indications seemed to confirm such a suspicion. The Franco-Belgians insisted with regard to private property that it be returned unconditionally, and would hear nothing of the counter-proposal by the terms of which the Russian government would keep the nationalised property and compensate the former owners with concessions or leases. This coincides in every detail with the attitude then and now of the Standard Oil and of the United States State Department.

It will serve the purpose of this argument now to touch upon the attitude of a very prominent publicist who was furthest from the British delegation, Wickham Steed, the editor of the London *Times*. The *Times*, which is a great political factor in English politics, had been consistently fighting Lloyd George. At the conference Mr. Steed remained faithful to this policy. Throughout the entire proceedings he frankly attacked the British policy and defended the Franco-Belgian. He was generally regarded as the mouthpiece of the French delegation, and so identical were his despatches with those of a Paris telegraphic agency that much suspicion was aroused and the matter was even discussed in the House of Commons. During the opening period of the conference he had consciously refrained from writing a word about the oil problem which Genoa had raised. To have done so might have revealed the true foundation of Franco-Belgian policy.

"But matters have now reached a point at which the oil question enters the political sphere. All the principal European delegations have received hints from the Ambassador of the United States that his government maintains its well-known standpoint in regard to any private or general arrangement made for commercial or industrial privileges in Russia and that no arrangement will be recognised by the United States." [11]

Mr. Child, the American ambassador in Rome, had

[11] The London *Times*, May 9th.

now arrived in Genoa, and lost no time in making his presence felt. He came as an "observer", which meant that he conducted all his activities behind the scenes by means of "hints" which, however, had the force of ultimatums. Especially the British government had learned from sad experience that the will of the United States government could not be thwarted in the matter of an "open door" for American oil companies. Downing Street had been taught that lesson in the eighteen months' conflict over the Mesopotamian petroleum fields, a conflict which had ended in a decisive victory for the State Department and the Standard Oil.[12] The economic and political influence of America had become too powerful since the war to be defied by any single nation or even combination of nations.

To return to Mr. Steed, his message continues as follows: "Whatever agreement has been or may be made must be affected by the American attitude unless and until the equality of industrial opportunity in Russia is assured on principles and by means which the United States can recognise. . . ."

Mr. Steed was well informed. He was also on close terms of intimacy with the French delegation. On the other hand, he was as far from the British delegation as any British correspondent could possibly have been, and as unalterably opposed to its policies. Yet we find him coming to the same conclusion as the correspondent of the *News of the World*, the confidant of the English delegates.

12 See chapter viii, "In the Shahdom of Persia".

"As regards the Standard Oil Company," writes Steed, "which wields great influence in the United States, it must be remembered that its acquisition of the oil rights of the Nobel Brothers in South Russia some time ago gives it a distinct status in Russian oil negotiations.

"This status clearly lends point to *the support given by the United States to the French and Belgian attitude in regard to private property in Russia*, as also to the polite invitation which the leading delegations here have received from the American ambassador." (Italics mine. L. F.)

In other words, the fact that the Standard Oil had purchased part of the Nobel holdings in Baku, lent point to the support given by the United States to France and Belgium at Genoa. Had not Mr. Steed's colleague hinted as much? [13]

Several days later (May 11th) Ambassador Child issued a statement which clearly enunciated the position of his government. "As to the petroleum question which has perhaps been exaggerated in the press controversies," the statement reads, "America as is her right and her duty, protects in Europe and elsewhere American citizens who have properties and rights that require protection. But the United States will never consent that any scheme whatsoever, national or inter-

[13] As early as March 15th, the Paris New York *Herald* was in a position to write that "Standard Oil interests are reported to be preparing to make a fight at Genoa to protect the company's old concessions, held in the name of the Russian Standard Oil Company, *and are seeking* French assistance against their British rival": the Shell. (Italics mine. L. F.)

national, shall be applied unless it takes account of the principle of the open door for all and recognised equal rights for all."

This declaration of the ambassador recalls the words of Mr. Bedford, of the Standard Oil, to the *Times* interviewer. And there was a very direct connection between it and the standpoint of the Standard Oil, for in the early days of the month Mr. Bedford had paid a visit to Secretary of State Hughes in Washington. Mr. Bedford reported his apprehension that America would be completely barred from the exploitation of the oil resources of Russia. But Hughes obligingly reassured the Standard Oil chief, and promised him that the United States would tolerate no agreement which would exclude American capital from Russian petroleum concessions.[14] Then came the Child statement.

Further light is thrown on Mr. Child's activities in Genoa by George Slocombe's despatch from Genoa to the London *Daily Herald* of May 15th. Mr. Slocombe discusses the proposals which had been advanced for the convening of a commission to examine the Russian question in The Hague. "These proposals," he wired, "though backed by M. Barthou, originated with Mr. Child, the American ambassador, evidently inspired by the Standard Oil interests. . . . To put the position in a few words: America had intervened in the Genoa Conference, and intervened in a sense hostile to the Soviets."

The Child-Barthou plan provided for the suspension

[14] The New York *Herald,* May 6, 1922.

of all treaties with Russia (including the Rapallo treaty with the Germans), and the representation of the United States but the exclusion of Russia from all committees which The Hague Conference was to set up on debts, private property, credits, etc. "This proposal," continues Slocombe, "was described by Chicherin to me yesterday as a return to the blockade of Russia."

The *Daily Herald* correspondent proceeds to quote Chicherin as follows: "The United States is the most hostile of all nations against us. And although the plan proposed by Child, with the support of Vanderlip and 'observers' of the Standard Oil now in Genoa, is disowned by Washington as unauthorised, it nevertheless represents the views of the American government and the basis on which it will participate in the commission to be set up at The Hague or elsewhere."

Mr. Child's activity was the *finita la comedia* of Genoa. Since the United States would not tolerate a concession to a British company, the Royal Dutch-Shell could accept none. The Bolsheviks now knew that they would not be the recipients of the credits and the recognition which the good-will of the Royal Dutch-Shell and therefore of the British government would have brought them. Moreover, the conference had reached an impasse: the Soviet delegation could not bow to the will of the French and the Belgians because that would have entailed the renunciation of some of the most fundamental precepts of Communist doctrine; there was no use agreeing to the British points of view because its chief purpose, a concession to the Royal Dutch, was unachievable. The Standard Oil had scored a victory. The policy of the company with regard to Russia was one of watchful waiting. It did not wish a concession under the terms upon which the Soviets were prepared to grant one. It felt that the time was not yet ripe for an agreement with Moscow, that the day would come when the Bolsheviks would be so hard pressed that they would either restore the Standard Oil's property in Baku or lease it to the "rightful" owner on conditions 100 per cent. favorable. But this policy would have become absolutely untenable the moment so powerful a company as the Royal Dutch-Shell signed a contract with the Russian government. Such an agreement would not merely have prejudiced the Standard Oil's case; it would have reinforced the Soviets economically and thus strengthened their resistance. This was the guiding motive of the Rockefeller firm in Genoa: there should be no attempt to agree with Russia now. At all costs other companies must be prevented from accepting a concession. It was this dog-in-the-manger method which wrecked the conference.

The Bolsheviks really closed the conference proceedings with their famous memorandum of May 11th in which they rejected the demands of the Allies in respect to private property. Thereafter Lloyd George, whose political future was to have been decided by the success or failure of Genoa, made some desperate efforts to keep the conference together. In vain, however. The Franco-Belgian bloc had won its point, or rather the point of the Standard Oil: there would be no agreement with and no concessions from the Soviets. Now they were anxious to quit the scene.

For several days the conference dragged out a miserable existence which had more resemblance to death than to life. In its dying struggles, however, the conference mustered enough strength to decide on resurrecting itself at The Hague within a month. The Hague meeting was to deal exclusively with the Russian problem. But because the realisation was general that no conference could achieve anything real and practical without the consent of the United States, it was decided to send an invitation to Washington. This, then, became the burning question: Would America participate?

And now, having gracefully performed the burial rites on May 19th, the diplomats retired to their several national capitals. Only the Bolsheviks stayed a week longer to keep a number of appointments with persistent capitalists, and to sign a separate treaty with the Italian government.

CHAPTER III

IN THE ROYAL DUTCH CAPITAL

THE Hague Conference was Genoa: continued. But during certain of its phases the stage setting was different and the relations between the several actor-nations underwent a change. Moreover, the individual *dramatis personæ* were not the same. Genoa had been honoured by the presence of the greatest stars in the diplomatic firmament: Lloyd George, Chicherin, Litvinov, Rathenau, Wirth, Benes, Barthou and others. At The Hague, on the contrary, the representatives of the Allied states were second and third class experts with limited *ad referendum* powers. Neither Lloyd Greame,[1] nor Alphand, nor Cattier, nor any of their colleagues were well known or very influential. But the big petroleum magnates appeared in force: Sir Henri Deterding, the president of the Royal Dutch trust; Sir Walter Samuel, the president of the Shell; Louis Lambo and Charles Laurent, vice-president and secretary, respectively, of the Franco-Belgian Syndicate, and a host of minor monarchs, not to mention Colonel Boyle, the Canadian engineer, who had played such a prominent rôle at Genoa, and representatives of the Standard Oil.

With respect to the activities of these petroleum men, the London *Oil News* of July 22, 1922, carries

[1] Now Sir Philip Cunliffe-Lister.

this caustic comment: "The Genoa Conference was remarkable for the number of important oil representatives present in its environs who one and all declared that they had not come there to talk with anybody concerning petroleum affairs. We hope that similar denials will not be forthcoming from The Hague, where oil representatives of a certain specified type and of cosmopolitan belongings have been observed to be busy."

The indefatigable Colonel Boyle, known for his daring rush to the Klondike gold region, took a suite in the hotel where rooms had been reserved for the delegates of the Russian Soviet Republic. Messrs. Deterding and Samuel tried to create the impression that they were in The Hague on current business details. But everybody knew that the liquid resources of the Caucasus interested these worthies much more than the Dutch landscape or the waves of Scheveningen.

From all appearances, the alignment of oil and diplomatic forces at The Hague gave promise of being no whit different from the alignment in Genoa. Indeed, the skirmishing which took place between the Quai D'Orsay and Downing Street before the heavy artillery gathered in the Royal Dutch capital seemed to improve such a prospect. On June 1st, for instance, the French Foreign Office despatched a memorandum to London which was practically nothing more than a résumé of the arguments advanced by Barthou at Genoa. Nine days later the British reply took sharp exception to some of the Parisian points.

"In the matter of private property, for instance,"

reads the English answer, "the French government contends that foreign claimants have the right to demand its return. . . . His Majesty's government cannot accept such a contention."

Nothing, apparently, had changed since the stormy days in the Italian conference city. More than that. The British were now more prepared than ever to stand their ground against the Franco-Belgian bloc, for their memorandum proceeds to defend that most radical of Bolshevik principles, the principle of expropriation. The English note to France affirms that "every state has the right compulsorily to acquire private property, whatsoever its nature, on payment of just compensation. . . . Whether the Russian government makes restitution of private property alienated from its owners, or pays compensation for it, is a matter solely for the Russian government."

Here, then, was a crystal-clear championship of the leasehold idea of the British in contradistinction to the Franco-Belgian-American idea of freehold and absolute restitution. In the intermission between Genoa and The Hague, no one, obviously, had been converted. This was the suspicious atmosphere in which the conference opened five days after the sentiments of the British Foreign Office had thus been set on paper.

The Hague Conference commenced its deliberations on June 15, 1922. On the very same day a highly important meeting took place in Paris. It was the organisation meeting of the Franco-Belgian Petrol Syndicate. The foundation of this syndicate had been laid at Genoa by an official representative of the French government, by M. Laurent-Eynac. Of his mission to the Genoa conference, M. Laurent-Eynac reports: "In the first place, we set on foot a plan for a union between the Belgian and French groups which will have two principal purposes: (1) the protection of rights acquired before the war as well as rights purchased subsequent to 1918 from the former proprietors, and (2) eventually, the concerted exploitation of the oil-fields which belong to the citizens of both nations." [2]

This union, which consisted largely of companies and groups that had bought Caucasian oil stocks on the Paris Bourse after the Russian oil-fields had been nationalised, took the form of the Franco-Belgian Syndicate. The chairman of the syndicate's organisation meeting was, be it remembered, none other than M. Pineau, director of the Essences and Petroles Service of the French Ministry of Commerce. He had accompanied M. Laurent-Eynac to Genoa and he was now in a position to assure the gathering that it enjoyed the good-will and patronage of the French government. It is important to note that the by-laws of the syndicate revealed the chief purpose of its existence to be the reacquisition of oil properties held by the Bolsheviks. Compensation was to be accepted only on rare occasions when no other solutions appeared possible.

One of the first steps of the new syndicate was to despatch "delegates" to The Hague Conference, delegates who "put themselves at the disposal of the French

[2] *Journée Industrielle,* May 20, 1922. Also *Matin* of May 19th.

and Belgian experts" in order to enlighten these on any developments of real importance and on the meaning of Soviet manœuvres.[3] This was the proper procedure. For who could instruct the semi-diplomatic experts better than oil men, and who had a clearer insight into the real purposes of the conference? At Genoa, high personalities, much news, many rumours, etc., had masked the true oleous face of the deliberations. But in the calm of The Hague, where the limelight on the conference stage was less blinding, and the noise of the coming and going of the great ones of the earth less deafening, there was a wider possibility of ascertaining the actual truth. Furthermore, disguises were less effective after the performance in Genoa. A few people, at least, realised that the loud rumble from the plenary sessions about which the dailies roared so much was perhaps less vital than the still small voice from behind the scenes.

For a week or so the conference followed an even, pleasant course. On June 26th, the Soviet plenipotentiaries arrived, led by Maxim Maximovitch Litvinov. The discussions on debts, loans, credits, which had been interrupted for more than a month were now renewed. To lose no time, Litvinov made the Russian attitude clear from the very outset. Before deliberating on the reconstruction of Russia and the part which foreign capital was to play in that process, before entering into any consideration of the properties which the Moscow government would restitute or indemnify, before discussing concessions to Allied capitalists, the

<hr>

[3] *Le Courrier des Petroles*, Paris, July 22, 1922.

Soviets, through Litvinov, wished to be given the assurance that Russia would receive a loan or credits or both. For Moscow this was the *sine qua non*. They needed and wanted money. Only if they got it would they be ready to talk business.

With the Russians obdurate, and the Allies in disagreement, a repetition in miniature of the farce of Genoa was generally expected. But one day, men with their ears close to the ground heard the shuffling and shifting of scenes backstage, and, suddenly, when the curtain rose again, John Bull, France and Belgium were discovered near the footlights dressed in smiles and exchanging kisses and embraces of concurrence. According to a second version, Uncle Sam was also among the players. He was seated on an oil can taking the first puff from a pipe of peace, and preparing to pass it on to his associates.

Evidence of an agreement soon made its appearance. On July 12th, for instance, Sir Philip Lloyd Greame, the head of the British delegation, declared at a meeting of the Private Property Sub-Commission, whose chairman he was, that: "It has been perfectly plain to everybody that the only effective form of compensation for seized property within the power of the Russian government to make at the present moment is the restitution of the property concerned wherever possible. We came here to learn what could be restored. . . ."

Sir Philip was here advocating the Franco-Belgian point of view. The British, obviously, had yielded. Between June 10th and July 12th something had happened. The London memorandum of June 10th told the French point blank that His Majesty's government was of the opinion that foreign claimants did not have the right to demand the restoration of their property. Yet on July 12th His Majesty's government's expert at The Hague insisted on the restoration of property in that he announced that the only acceptable form of compensation was restitution. Rather than yield one inch of the British position at Genoa on the question of Compensation *vs*. Restitution, Lloyd George permitted the conference, which was to have been the crowning glory of his political career, to end in dismal failure. The British Prime Minister had endangered the Entente and risked incurring the enmity of France, yet surrender an iota he would not. And his Cabinet's antagonism to the Franco-Belgian programme of the restoration of property alienated by the Bolsheviks continued for at least another month. It had undergone no change as late as June 10th. Then of a sudden, London executed a complete and surprising *volte face*, and adopted the Paris-Brussels viewpoint adding only a meaningless, mildly conditional "whenever possible".

One may search the minutes of the plenary sessions of The Hague Conference; one may study the protocols of every meeting of its several commissions and subcommissions. No explanation of this strange surrender on the part of the British will be found.

It may be supposed that the English had previously been ignorant of Russian conditions and learned only subsequently, at The Hague, that the Bolsheviks were in no position to compensate the former owners. Therefore they now insisted on restoration as the only practical solution of the situation. But such a supposition would be incorrect. All the delegations at Genoa were well informed on the state of affairs in the Soviet Republic. They had their agents there, and besides, the newspapers, particularly the British newspapers, regularly printed the picture of Red Russia in darkest black. Moreover, the Bolsheviks made no secret of their hardships and necessity either at Genoa or at The Hague. As a matter of fact, Russia's very acceptance of the Allied invitation to send plenipotentiaries to the Genoa conference stated that it would probably be impossible for Lenin to attend on account of the famine which had undermined the economic structure of the country and necessitated the lifesaving activity of Hoover's American Relief Administration. No. The clue to the British riddle must be sought elsewhere.

It must be sought, along with the explanation of many more of the most important developments of The Hague Conference, in the proceedings of the unofficial, but very decisive, oil parley held simultaneously with the official Conference. Regarding this important "side-show", Davenport and Cooke, in their interesting volume on *The Oil Trusts and Anglo-American Relations*, write as follows:

"It should be mentioned that the 'oil entente' which suddenly sprang up at Genoa between the French and the Belgians in the face of the pretended danger from the Shell-Soviet scheme, developed later at the French government's suggestion, into the then 'Syndicat Franco-Belge' for the protection of French and Belgian interests in the Russian oil industry. This syndicate sent 'delegates' to The Hague, and behind the official doors conversations followed with Sir Henri Deterding and other representatives of the Royal Dutch-Shell combination. One fancies that *this was The Hague Conference which really mattered.*" (Italics mine. L. F.)

Messrs. Davenport and Cooke are highly respectable English gentlemen, yet they fancy that what Lloyd Greame, M. Cattier and the other spokesmen of the great Powers said and did at the sessions of the committees and commissions was of no importance at all compared with the little private talks between persons who spoke only in the name of a few directors of petroleum companies. The indications are that the two authors were right.

It will be recalled that the merger type of concession, in favour of which the Bolsheviks have a natural prejudice, had failed to provide the basis for an agreement in Genoa. The Soviet delegation tried a different tack at The Hague. The new course was announced by Litvinov on July 7th at a joint meeting of the Private Property Sub-Commission, the most important organ of the conference, with the Soviet delegation.

"Sir Philip Lloyd Greame was in the chair. M. Litvinov explained the conditions on which concessions would be granted to private capitalists, and read a list of properties, *notably oil-fields* [Italics mine.

L. F.], in respect of which concessions could be arranged." [4]

The document read by Litvinov is attached as an annex to the protocol of the sub-commission's session. The concession he adumbrated on the occasion covered parts of unexploited oil-fields as well as of old fields in Baku, Grosni, Emba, Kuban, Turkestan and Ferghana. The policy enunciated at the session did not, however, signify that the Russians contemplated returning unto each company the property which it had once held in South Russia. Nothing of the kind. It merely meant that the Moscow authorities would deal with single applicants for concessions and give them a choice of certain, enumerated parcels of oil-bearing land upon which their bidding might be concentrated. Former owners as well as interests which had had no holdings at all were eligible for this grand contest, although groups in the first category would, in view of their experience and special claims, be likely to receive a better hearing. Under no condition, however, would the Soviet consent to outline a blanket set of rules on the basis of which any concessions candidate could procure a lease. Each application would be examined separately in Moscow, and judged there on its own merits, the final decision depending to a great extent on the attitude of the authorities to the individual company-applicant.

This Bolshevik proposal satisfied no one. The British as well as the French and Belgians were united in opposing it. And naturally, for it bound the Soviet

[4] London *Times,* July 8, 1922.

government to little and merely promised difficulties to the oil concerns. The immediate effect, therefore, of Litvinov's announcement was the cementing of the Allied ranks. It achieved the unity and agreement among the Western Powers of which the July 12th statement by Sir Philip Lloyd Greame was but an echo.

This unity at the official conference was, needless to say, merely a reflection of the consensus of opinion which prevailed at "The Hague Conference which really mattered". This oil confab had been convened by Sir Henri Deterding "through the President of The Hague Conference and the various delegations". Such, at least, was the assertion of the Paris *Temps*. But whether or not the official Hague Conference itself sponsored the unofficial one from which it took its cues, the fact is that the oil parley did take place. Deterding acted as chairman. Sir Henri, incidentally, was on home ground at The Hague, for though his citizenship is English, his firm under English control, and his title the gift of His Britannic Majesty, Henri Wilhelm August, like the company he directs, is of Dutch origin, and it is perhaps not altogether accidental that the official as well as the unofficial Conference assembled in one of the two metropoles of the great Anglo-Dutch trust.

The Royal Dutch-Shell was of course anxious to arrive at a settlement with the Soviet government. As subsequent events proved this was certainly the better part of wisdom. If the oil magnates had known in 1922 what they know now they would undoubtedly have followed Mr. Deterding's advice and footsteps instead of placing obstacles in his path. But in this case, hope and faith,—hope and faith in the fall or ultimate yielding of the Soviets,—were bad business partners. They misled industrialists, financiers and people whom we generally regard as very astute into losing hundreds of millions of dollars. We cannot say whether it was out of supreme cleverness or out of a desire to steal a march on its arch rival, the Standard Oil, that the Royal Dutch persisted in its sensible attitude of treating with the Bolsheviks. History, however, must surely award the crown to Sir Henri.

Nevertheless, in face of the Russian proposal of July 7th, Mr. Deterding was powerless. All the oil men were solidly against him. A Hague correspondent of the *Courrier des Petroles* describes as follows one of the sessions of the petrol conference which deliberated upon the Soviet suggestion:

". . . last week," he writes, "a meeting of special representatives of foreign investors in Russian oil took place at The Hague, at which were present French, Belgian and British interests. It had just come to their notice that the Soviets had issued a printed document wherein they stated their willingness to grant concessions over certain blocks of oil lands, the property of various firms, whereupon the British representatives present, M. H. G. Trew, of the Spies Petroleum Company, Ltd., and Mr. Richard R. Tweed, of the Baku Consolidated Oil-fields, Ltd., proposed to their French and Belgian friends that a meeting should be held immediately to make a public statement refusing, under any circumstances, to take concessions over property belonging to other people. Further any effort they might make would be directed entirely to obtaining the return of their own property or compensation for same."

The opposition of Messrs. Tweed and Trew to the Soviet concession policy is noteworthy. At the Genoa conference, Mr. Trew had attempted to obstruct the Shell monopoly contract, and sought to mobilise the Belgians and French in his cause. For in this matter the small British companies over which Messrs. Tweed and Trew presided, as well as the Franco-Belgians, were the natural allies of the Standard Oil. A concession to the Shell would have eliminated the Spies and Baku Consolidated Companies, or at best put them at the mercy of Sir Henri. It would similarly have put at a decided disadvantage those many French and Belgian interests which, like the Standard Oil, had acquired their claims to oil-fields in the Caucasus subsequent to the Bolshevik Nationalisation Act of 1918.

This united front of the small British owners, and the post-1918 interests, had paralysed the Shell's efforts at Genoa. Its recrudescence at The Hague again checkmated the Deterding corporation. Against it all Sir Henri's sagacity was of no avail. Moreover, the Royal Dutch could really not wax enthusiastic over a plan which promised the company much less than the project it had superseded.

But, by the time the news of the attitude of the petroleum representatives commenced trickling out into the press, often in garbled form, the Bolsheviks had already taken up another position. Or rather, they had returned to the position abandoned by them after the failure of Genoa: they resurrected the formula of a merger-monopoly concession.

"The Bolshevik spokesman today," reads a Hague telegram to the London *Daily Telegraph* of July 18th, "made an important admission that Russia, instead of returning the various oil properties to their original owners, intended to form one general company to carry on all operations. The oil company which gets the contract to operate all the oil-fields will be asked to satisfy the other claimants."

This announcement had all the earmarks of Russia's concessions policy. The Moscow leaders prefer to avoid the responsibility of dealing with and the trouble of being bothered by numerous groups which may have a claim or think they have a claim, upon some property in Soviet Russia. Nor does the Russian government have any special desire to recognise the rights of former owners over nationalised wealth. It has never done so directly even unto this day. In 1922 the Bolsheviks were disposed in favour of a blanket concession to one foreign entrepreneur who, it was taken for granted, would satisfy the claims of any former owners whose effects may have been leased to him by the Russian state. They have a similar preference now. The 1925 agreement with W. A. Harriman, of New York, giving him an invaluable contract to the manganese ore deposits in Chiaturi, the richest in the world, is a concession of just this nature. Harriman had never had any interests in Chiaturi. On the other hand, some twenty-five foreign companies had owned mines there before the revolution and had worked on them until 1925. When Harriman appeared on the scene to bid for the manganese fields he was, in effect, offering to oust and dispossess all the other concerns which had been operating there for a score of years or more. This did not deter the Chief Concessions Committee in Moscow. It gave the lease to Mr. Harriman. And Harriman, who as a capitalist could hardly assume the rôle of an expropriator of other capitalists, was forced to make his own private settlement with the several firms to whose tracts he had obtained title. The Soviets thus spared themselves money, political complications and the necessity of affirming the pre-war rights of foreigners over property in Russia.

If the Bolsheviks would have had their way in The Hague, the Royal Dutch-Shell would have been the first Harriman. Mr. Deterding's firm would have received a concession covering oil-fields which many large and tiny petroleum companies had owned in the ante-revolutionary era. All of these the Anglo-Dutch trust would have had to placate, either by paying them off or taking them into the new business.

The retraction by the Soviets of their proposal to grant many concessions to many companies and their resurrection of the earlier project of an all-inclusive, merger lease was a call to arms to the Royal Dutch. Being the most likely candidate for this attractive concession, it immediately proceeded to establish contact with the French, Belgian and minor British interests with a view to winning them for the new scheme. For experience at Genoa had shown that no settlement could be reached over the heads of the French and Belgians. Here we enter into the second phase of "The Hague Conference which really mattered".

In this phase, Sir Henri Deterding's primary task was to wean the Franco-Belgians from their opposition to a Russian settlement. If he could manage to align them on his side by offering them participation in the exploitation of the oil-fields which the Bolsheviks were presumably prepared to lease to his company, the Standard Oil would lose the "Prætorian Guard" which fought its battles at European conferences. He must have been convinced that if he could achieve Anglo-French-Belgian agreement on the Caucasus question nothing would separate him from a contract. For such a triple combination, he probably thought, would be strong and courageous enough to defy the United States. Perhaps even, his secret intention (the Soviets willing) was later to throw a bone to the Standard Oil, too, but then only on his own terms, for the Royal Dutch and the Standard Oil were life-and-death enemies, and Sir Henri was certainly too shrewd to share on equal bases all the advantages which his persistence and strategy might bring him.

According to one rumour,[5] it seems that from the very beginning the Belgians were rather cold to Sir Henri's advances, but the attitude of the French, which was more favourable, later weakened their opposition.

France's oil policy during the period under discussion was necessarily vacillating. Before the war, France had had no policy with respect to petroleum.

[5] *Courrier des Petroles,* July 22, 1922.

She possessed very little oil at home and there were few important French companies which operated abroad. As to the domestic market, it was almost entirely in the hands of the Royal Dutch-Shell. The position of the Anglo-Dutch combine was further strengthened by the fact that the Rothschild Frères from whom, it will be recalled, the Deterding firm had purchased its holdings in the Caucasus, acted as the company's Paris banker;—and the Rothschilds were a mighty power.

The San Remo agreement of April, 1920, still further identified French oil politics with British oil interests.[6] By virtue of that accord, both signatory Powers agreed to share and divide certain petroleum resources in various parts of the globe. But actually it was the British who were signing away sections of oil lands which its armies had conquered. Particularly was this the case in Mesopotamia. There were thus plenty of good reasons for a common Anglo-French oil policy.

On the other hand, the Cadman negotiations with the Standard Oil in 1921 [7] made that organisation a partner to France and England in Mosul. Indeed, the Cadman Pact had the effect of identifying the Standard Oil with the San Remo agreement as far as Iraq was concerned. Thereafter, accordingly, France

[6] The San Remo agreement contains the following article [6] on the question of the Russian oil-fields:
"In the territories which belonged to the late Russian Empire, the two governments [the French and the British] will give their joint support to their respective nationals in their joint efforts to obtain petroleum concessions and facilities to export, and to arrange the delivery of petroleum supplies."
[7] See chapter viii, "In the Shahdom of Persia".

was able to orient herself either after England and the Royal Dutch, or the United States and the Standard Oil. To increase this possibility of an alternative, conditions in the French domestic oil market had undergone a change. Before 1914 the supremacy of the Royal Dutch was practically undisputed. But the war gave the American trust an advantage. The late Lord Curzon once remarked very aptly that "the Allies floated to victory on waves of oil", but he failed to mention that the oil was American oil. In answer to Clémenceau's frantic appeal to Woodrow Wilson in March, 1918, hundreds of tankers crossed the ocean to fill empty reservoirs in Flanders and France. It was American petroleum which moved the Allied aeroplanes, tanks and motor lorries in the last decisive months of the world struggle. And while this activity of the Standard Oil was proceeding, the company was building itself a berth in France; establishing connections, erecting tanks, gaining favour with officials, etc. The hostilities over, the war gains served as a foundation for peacetime business benefits. For a while Royal Dutch influence, supported by the French government, resisted the encroachment of the American trust. Soon enough, however, the Standard was a serious competitor of the Shell. In 1920, the Standard Franco-Americaine was formed under the directorship of General Gassouin, formerly of the French General Staff, who cooperated with Pineau and Laurent-Eynac in Genoa. In the autumn of the succeeding year when Mr. Bedford visited Paris it became known that the French Standard was allied to the Banque de Paris, one of the most powerful commercial banks in Europe. Gradually, this new agency acquired more and more of the custom of the Royal Dutch. But aside from the increasing economic strength of this new Rockefeller branch, France's moral, military and above all, financial indebtedness to the United States tended to give a handicap to the American oil company. With the enormous prestige gained by the United States since the World War, American firms abroad, whether or not they enjoy the active or passive support of the State Department, are almost invariably at an advantage.

There were then two petrol giants competing for supremacy in France: the Royal Dutch-Shell combine, old, established, its hold slowly acquired; and the Standard Oil, youthful, aggressive, its position recently attained yet favoured by a number of important circumstances in world finance and politics.

However, it was not only in France that these two trusts engaged in bitter competition. In Mexico they struggle for supremacy. In South America, the Royal Dutch is an active rival of its North American enemy. Even in the United States proper, the Royal Dutch mines, refines, carries and sells oil in quantities large enough to perturb the House of Rockefeller. On every foreign market the two oil mammoths collide with one another. China is a historic example. The struggle over Russian oil at Genoa and The Hague was thus only a part, a very important part, of the far-flung, world-wide war between the Royal Dutch and the Standard.

At Genoa the Standard Oil had achieved victory largely by mobilising France and Belgium in its support. The Royal Dutch now mustered every effort to prevent a similar combination at The Hague. Deterding's company was not without influence in Paris and Brussels. Besides Sir Henri had a very practical proposition to place before the "delegates" of the Franco-Belgian Syndicate. He could offer them a parcel of stock in the concessions company which he would form for Russia. This would have been a sop to silence the syndicate's opposition and to anticipate any embarrassment to the British government which, by reason of the San Remo agreement, was under obligation to accord fair treatment to French petrol interests.

For a few days the French wavered and then, pressed by Deterding, they seemed inclined to accept. They had much to gain from a Russian settlement. At any rate this is very obvious now when the several companies sit in London, Paris, Brussels, etc., nursing their worthless stock while the Soviet government exploits all oil property in Russia, including the property of these companies, and sells the product on the world market, much to the profit of its exchequer.

If any of the "delegates" of the Franco-Belgian Syndicate saw even most faintly what the future might bring we can well understand their readiness to compromise on "principles" and by-laws, and follow the lead of the Royal Dutch. Or did they fear the wrath of the Standard Oil whose chestnuts they had picked at Genoa? Or did the French government, perhaps, and the Belgian government, perhaps, fear the wrath of the American State Department. The Franco-Belgians, at any rate, hesitated and cogitated. But in the meantime a direct wire had, so to speak, been erected between The Hague Conference and Washington. There was much coming and going at the United States ministry in the Royal Dutch capital.

Now we may return to the official conference of experts. Just as circumstances had forced the Russians to bow to the unanimous will of the oil men on the concessions question, so the stubborn opposition of the governments in the matter of debts compelled them to change their tactics in this field as well. They had come to The Hague proclaiming that unless they received loans or credits or both they would neither recognise nor pay their debts. But the Allies were not prepared to advance money to the Bolsheviks. Nevertheless, Litvinov and his colleagues were bent on some kind of an agreement. An agreement would strengthen them at home, increase their prestige abroad, and what was more important, bring them business and foreign capital. Here it seemed as if the Royal Dutch would round up the smaller fellows and thus remove the difficulties which stood in the way of their concession. Yet the Russians would have had to grant that concession without the loan and credits on which they had made it conditional. This Litvinov could not do on his own authority. His instructions were to compromise on debts and hand out concessions provided he could bring home a loan. But seeing that the loan was not forthcoming, he had to consult Moscow. Accordingly

Litvinov informed the conference on July 19th that he would wire to his government for new instructions. It did not lie within his prerogative to decide on so radical a departure in Soviet policy. He would enquire from his superiors whether he might proceed with the negotiations on debts, compensation and concessions, even if no money were offered by the Allied countries.

This was a perfectly normal and natural step to take. Nor did the Allied representatives dissuade Litvinov from his intention. *But on the very next day, without waiting for the reply from Moscow, they hastily, at the suggestion of the Sub-Commission on Private Property, convened a plenary session of the non-Russian delegations and declared the conference closed.*

The rôle of the Sub-Commission on Private Property at The Hague Conference was characterised in the statement which Litvinov made before the Council of People's Commissars in Moscow. "The uncompromising attitude of the Sub-Commission on Private Property of the Non-Russian Commission, which influenced the decisions of the other sub-commissions as well, was the chief cause of the failure of the entire conference. In this way the interests of the economic rehabilitation of Russia and Europe, and the interests of the overwhelming mass of the small holders of Russian state bonds were sacrificed to the interests of a comparatively small group of powerful former private property owners." The "powerful former private property owners" were, of course, the oil magnates.

So strange a demarche as the sudden closing of the

conference only a day after the Russians had announced the possibility of a far-reaching compromise could have been justified only by very unusual and compelling circumstances. The last minutes of the proceedings offer a clue as to what these were. The final act of The Hague Conference was the adoption of a resolution which read:

"The conference recommends for the consideration of the governments represented thereon the desirability of all governments not assisting their nationals in attempting to acquire property in Russia which belonged to other foreign nationals and which was confiscated since November 1, 1917, without the consent of such foreign owners or concessionaires, provided that the same recommendation is subsequently made by governments represented at The Hague Conference to all governments not so represented, and that no decision shall be come to except jointly with those governments." In other words, it ruled out the Royal Dutch monopolistic concession which would have covered property belonging to nationals of countries other than Great Britain. M. Cattier, the Belgian delegate who moved the resolution, stated that the United States government approved of its contents and had authorised him to make a public announcement to that effect.

This resolution was the only concrete result of The Hague Conference. And is it not significant that the American government, which had not participated in the conference, should have seen fit to add the weight of its influence to a move which prevented a Russian settlement? After all, if the United States was interested in the Russian question it might have sat at the conference. It had been invited. If, however, it was not concerned, why did it inject itself into the final, decisive session? This was most uncommon diplomatic usage.

M. Cattier had been in touch with the American minister at The Hague during the greater part of the conference. Several experienced journalists who reported the conference proceedings were of the opinion that the Cattier resolution against Russian concessions had actually been drafted in Washington and then been forwarded to the United States minister who placed it in the hands of the Belgian delegate for submission to the Allied representatives. Be that as it may, the resolution certainly expressed the wishes of the Standard Oil Company in respect to Soviet oil concessions. This time America had "turned the trick" without even sending an "observer" to the conference.

America could have had only a single interest in The Hague Conference's final resolution. That was oil. United States nationals owned very little property in Russia before the revolution, and such as it was,—a factory of the International Harvester and another belonging to Westinghouse, the Soviets had never nationalised it. American intervention at The Hague can, therefore, be explained simply and solely by the State Department's desire to protect the questionable claims of the Standard Oil Company on Baku.

CHAPTER IV

THE OIL BLOCKADE AND AFTER

THE historic resolution adopted on the last day of The Hague Conference was the fitting preliminary to a universal blockade against Russian oil and Soviet concessions. A *cordon sanitaire* would be built about Russia. No one would buy her oil or apply for her concessions. Having no other alternative, she would be forced to yield and return the petroleum properties to their former owners.

On July 24th and 25th, only a few days after the sudden end of The Hague Conference, the press carried statements about a possible general world oil congress. A week later the situation had become more definite and the *Courrier des Petroles* of August 5th was able to announce that "in the coming September a conference in Paris will unite the holders of oil rights in Russia of all nationalities under the ægis of the French government." The September 9th issue of the same oil paper affirmed that "the foreigners have decided to form a block and not permit themselves to be disunited by separate attractive offers," a thrust at the Royal Dutch.

Meanwhile the Standard Oil Company encouraged the formation of a united anti-Soviet front. Its president, apparently, was particularly anxious to pin down Mr. Deterding's corporation. "It is evident,"

Mr. Teagle is quoted as saying,[1] "that no English company is going to negotiate today with the Russians on its own account. It is also clear that as long as the Russian government will not have returned to the foreign proprietors their properties in Russia or will not have accorded them compensation at the same time guaranteeing the security of private property in Russia, no resumption of safe business with Russia is possible, and no new investment for oil exploitation in Russia can securely be made."

The heralded conference took place in September in Paris.   There were present delegates of the Royal Dutch, the Standard Oil, Anglo-Persian, the Franco-Belgian Syndicate, also of a number of purely Russian companies such as Lianosov, Mantashev, etc.   The Standard Oil was represented by Gustav Nobel, the Royal Dutch by Sir Henri Deterding.   Sir Henri, the "Napoleon of Petroleum", presided.

It was not without interest that Deterding wielded the gavel at this meeting.   For the oil firms were scheming to force the Royal Dutch into assuming the leadership of a movement to which it was fundamentally opposed and in which it participated only half-heartedly.   The real object of the conference was to tame the Royal Dutch, which alone among the petroleum powers would not desist from its efforts to regain a foothold in the Caucasus.   And what better modus could there be of binding the Royal Dutch than of setting it up as the sponsor, guardian and protector of the blockade?

[1] *Courrier des Petroles,* September 2, 1922.

The meeting organised itself into the *Groupement International des Sociétés Naphtières en Russie,* or "Groupement" as it is commonly known. The several companies retained their individuality as business concerns, but in all matters relating to their Russian affairs they pledged themselves to act as a unit and never independently of one another.

The basic principles of the Groupement were laid down in the protocol of the first meeting which reads as follows: "Upon the invitation of the Royal Dutch-Shell group and the Nobel Brothers, there assembled in Paris on the 19th of September, 1922, under the chairmanship of Sir Henri Deterding, unanimously elected as president, the representatives of eighteen Russian and foreign societies which have previously been operating in Russia.

"Representing the great majority of the interests engaged in the oil industry and trade in the former Russian Empire, those present declared that they form a united front for the defence of the rights and interests of that industry. Those present agreed and definitely approved and accepted in their own as well as in the name of their subsidiaries the declarations of the representatives of the Royal Dutch-Shell which are summarised thus:

"(1) It is inadmissible for any of the interested parties present directly or indirectly to act against the existing interests and acquired rights of other proprietors dispossessed by Soviet legislation.

"(2) Exploitation of the oil-fields is possible only upon the condition of the reintegration and rehabilitation on equal conditions to all the interested parties of their rights and properties.

"(3) The oil-fields belonging to the state represent a common fund necessary to the full development of the oil industry, and as such they must not be accepted by any of the interested parties as an individual concession without an agreement by all the parties."

The Groupement's Three Commandments, everyone must agree, were not intended to bring about an understanding with Soviet Russia but rather to prevent one. If any company could settle its claims with the Russian government it was to forego the advantage and wait till all its associates, in the Groupement united, had obtained similar satisfaction. If the Soviets offered a group a concession to a field on which there was no claim, either Russian or foreign, because it had never been in private ownership, it was to be refused outright. Obviously, the question was no more one of compensation or restitution. A stronger slogan was raised: Blockade and Boycott. Even if the Russians desired to compensate some of the companies, even if the Russians desired to restitute some property, the Groupement members would answer with an emphatic "No." The object was now to force the Bolsheviks to capitulate, to bring them to their knees. Then it would be no longer a matter of pourparlers and discussions. The victorious Groupement would dictate the terms on which the former dispossessed owners were to march back to their oil-fields in the Caucasus.

This was a triumph for the Standard Oil viewpoint and a defeat for that of Royal Dutch. Yet the Royal

Dutch accepted the situation stoically and even administered the whipping to its own self. Practically, there was nothing else to do—not at that moment.

The Groupement enlisted oil companies of six nationalities: American, British, French, Belgian, Dutch and Russian. The French and Belgians, the militant exponents of the organisation, were the most zealous advocates of the Blockade and Boycott idea. The United States interests, on the other hand, maintained a rather cold and suspecting attitude. It was probably because they felt themselves uncomfortable in Royal Dutch society. Perhaps, even, they did not trust Mr. Deterding and declined, therefore, to let their enthusiasm commit them.

The jealousy between the Standard and the Royal Dutch-Shell was one of the elements which, from the very beginning, militated against a success of the united front tactics of the Groupement. Another was the opposition to the Russians on the part of the purely foreign companies. It was argued by such organisations as the Spies Petroleum Company of Great Britain, and by the British Baku Consolidated, Ltd., which did not join the Groupement, that the admission of the Russians undermined the case of the foreign owners. The Russians were in a separate category, for it was argued, a government had a right to sequester the properties and wealth of its nationals as it sees fit. The Russians in the Groupement would, therefore, become the most vulnerable sectors in the united front which, if it consisted only of non-Russians, had precedent and international law on its side. This argument was certainly plausible and cogent. But how could the Standard Oil admit it when its rights in Baku arose out of its transaction with Nobel, a Russian citizen? Or how could Deterding allow such a contention when he had bought out Mantashev, Lianosov and other Russians? And what of the French who had purchased Russian paper on the stock exchange? The selfish interests of the several members of the Groupement thus early prejudiced the success of the entire manœuvre.

But it was not so much their selfish interests as their selfish and competitive tendencies which were most likely to ruin the Groupement.

The special function of the militant Franco-Belgians consisted in watching these tendencies and to bark as soon as any danger came nigh. They did not wait long for an opportunity. In February, 1923, about four months after the organisation of the Groupement, rumours began to spread that the Royal Dutch had made a deal with the Soviet government. It had indeed. Mr. Deterding could contain himself no longer. He had bought some kerosene which the Bolsheviks had produced in Baku. He was a "traitor" to the cause of Blockade and Boycott.

The London *Petroleum Times* of May 26, 1923, tells the whole story with all the intriguing details.

"The affair of the purchase of 70,000 tons of Russian oil," writes the Paris correspondent of the journal, "with an option for a further 100,000 tons, is still rankling, and some of our papers are making serious reflections upon the tactics of the Royal Dutch Company. Everyone knows, of course, of the Franco-Belgian Syndicate of September, 1922 [the Groupement] members of which undertook to refuse to do anything which would directly or indirectly injure the interests and rights of firms or persons who had been dispossessed of their property by the Russian Soviets, that no exploitation of Russian properties should be undertaken until the Soviets had made restitution; and that the State properties should not be subject to any 'individual concessions' without common agreement. It is affirmed that the Royal Dutch representatives were the most eager [sic] to encourage in every way possible the boycott of the Russian oils, yet at a meeting [of the Groupement] in Paris on March 26th they informed their fellow members that they had decided to purchase certain stocks of oil in order to protect them from 'spoiling the market', and they considered that in this way they were not violating the agreement, as it 'referred to the oil-fields and not to production.' The syndicate [Groupement] was astounded at this form of logic, and said that there could be no interest in the ground without the products, and that in any case *to buy products from the Soviets was simply supplying them with funds to continue their nefarious policy of confiscation.* [Italics mine. L. F.] In the end the syndicate [Groupement] 'invited' the Royal Dutch to refuse to take up the option for the 100,000 tons, and also to cancel their firm purchase of 70,000 tons. With a view to appeasing the wrath of their fellow members, the Royal Dutch Company's representatives offered to share its purchases with the syndicate. This was refused, and the feeling that the Royal Dutch had acted disloyally towards the syndicate was not improved by the discovery later on that the agreement of purchase, said to have been signed on March 2nd, was really only signed on March 29th—three days after the meeting."

All's fair in war—and in the oil business. The fact was that the Royal Dutch had broken the pledge it gave on adhering to the Groupement, and the above recital records that the company's representatives told a lie to boot. The excuse given sounds rather lame. It is true that an independent company was buying Russian oil and that the Soviet product was finding its way into the British market. But even from the strict business point of view, the action of the Royal Dutch was hardly justifiable; from the "moral" side it certainly was not.

However, such "disloyalty" might have been expected from the Royal Dutch. The firm had never been fully in sympathy with the blockade programme. It had consistently favoured trade relations with the Soviets. If it sinned by signing a contract with Moscow, that was its real nature taking the upper hand over temporarily assumed politeness.

But what of the Standard Oil? The American trust was the mightiest and loudest champion of the boycott principle. The "Hands Off Red Oil" device was writ large on its banner. Yet in the very winter, perhaps in the very month when Sir Henri Deterding's inferiors were bargaining with the Arcos [2] in London, Mr. Dodge, an official of the Standard Oil Company, was in Moscow. I had the pleasure of talking with him there. He came not merely to buy oil. That was the minor offence of the Royal Dutch-Shell. He came to get a concession. We shall return to this concession in another chapter. For the moment it suffices to note that within a half year after the solid petroleum Groupement front had been established with the avowed aim of besieging the Soviets until they were reduced, two—the largest two—of the interests had deserted the ranks and were sabotaging the cause for which they had agreed to fight. It was, however, a peculiar form of desertion that permitted these organisations to adhere to the Groupement whose members were forbidden all intercourse with the Soviets, and at the same time to make business arrangements or try to make business arrangements with the anathemised Bolsheviks. They simultaneously besieged the city and broke bread with the citizens within the walls.

One of the most striking illustrations of the fickleness of oil men was supplied by the directors of the Spies Petroleum Co. which before the revolution had had considerable holdings in Grosni. Mr. Gwynne Trew, the president of the company, admits that at Genoa he was extremely active in opposing the efforts of the Royal Dutch to obtain a concession, and in mobilising the French and Belgians against a Russian settlement. He played a similar rôle at The Hague Con-

[2] The Arcos Company, Ltd., is a Soviet buying and selling organisation in Great Britain.

ference, that is, in July, 1922. But in August he and some of his associates were in Berlin negotiating with Soviet authorities about a concession. So also, incidentally, were agents of the Belgian Akverdov corporation. The next month he appeared in Paris as one of the organisers of the Groupement whose members were never to touch a Soviet concession or talk to the Russians individually. Yet on November 20th, the Spies directors decided to resume relations with the Moscow government independent of the Groupement, and in November, too, the Spies Petroleum wrote a lengthy letter to Stomonyakov, the Russian Trade Envoy in Berlin, in which it was definitely proposed that the company was "willing to return to Russia at the earliest possible moment with our organisation and to provide fresh capital which may be necessary for the resumption of our not unhonourable connection with the Russian oil industry."

"The moment has now arrived," continues the letter, "for serious negotiations." Yet at that very moment the Spies Company was still a member of the Groupement's boycotting united front.

One might have expected at least the French to remain loyal. But, on August 23rd and 24th the Groupement met in Deauville under the chairmanship of Sir Henri Deterding to "consider the reported 'tentatives' which had been made by certain French personalities to obtain petroleum concessions in Russia. *It was decided to draw the attention of the French government to the danger of such negotiations.*" [3]   (Italics mine.

[3] *Petroleum Times,* September 22, 1923.

L. F.) Conjure up the picture of Sir Henri sitting in judgment over other transgressors.

The "personalities" referred to were agents of the Omnium International de Petrole, a French company generally regarded as a Standard Oil subsidiary.

These "French personalities" who were bidding for state oil properties in Russia and not for private, nationalised fields, had consummated a radical modification of the French government's policy. This appears from the Groupement's letter of September 6, 1923, to M. Pineau, the official petrol commissar.

"In his capacity as delegate of the Franco-Belgian Syndicate," reads this communication which is signed by thirty-two companies, "and as a member of our group, M. Charles Laurent states that he has your authority to inform us that you do not share our opinion relative to the so-called 'state' petroleum fields of Russia, and that you consider these fields can be made the object of contract between new groups on the one hand and the Soviet authorities on the other.

"After a thorough examination of this question, our group considers it desirable to draw your attention to the fact that Paragraph 3 of our constitutional resolutions regarding these oil-fields is in *exact conformity with the spirit of the resolutions which were firmly supported by the French and Belgian governments at the Genoa and Hague conferences.*" [4] (Italics mine. L. F.)

---

[4] This paragraph reads: "The oil-fields belonging to the state represent a common fund necessary to the full development of the oil industry, and, as such they must not be accepted by any

The Groupement's protest was an interesting contribution to the source material on the history of international conferences, but it accomplished nothing. The spirit of the Groupement was now thoroughly demoralised. The cause had been betrayed by large and small companies, and now by its potent patron, the French state. But a greater blow was still in store. It came at the meeting of the Groupement held on September 25, 1923—just a year after its birth.

Inevitably, Mr. Deterding presided. According to the very well-informed Paris correspondent of the *Petroleum Times* [5] "the group came to the decision that immediate negotiations should be entered into with the Soviet government with regard to the various oilfield properties in Russia and their exploitation. . . ."

"So," comments the correspondent, "the famous resolution of September, 1922, which, as the *Temps* said, 'needed no development nor lent itself to any equivocation', has gone the way of many other good resolutions."

This resolution was tantamount to the voluntary dissolution of the Groupement. The "traitor", who but a few months previously was savagely raked over the coals for buying kerosene from the Soviets, had persuaded his critics that "business is business" even when moral issues are involved, and that it was better to discuss matters with Moscow than to nurse a theoretic principle while practical opportunities were slipping by.

of the interested parties as an individual concession without an agreement by all the parties."

[5] October 13, 1923.

Needless to say, many Groupement members were displeased with the resolution to negotiate with the Bolsheviks. Accordingly, they formed "The Inter-Allied Committee of Oil Companies in Russia". This occurred during the latter half of October, 1923; in other words, it followed immediately upon the triumph of the Royal Dutch idea in the Groupement. British, French, Belgian and Russia firms adhered to the new body, which, however, was much weaker and much less impressive than the parent organisation. The bolters adopted by-laws identical with those which had been violated by the Groupement.

The rupture in the Groupement did not worry Sir Henri. Indeed, it almost certainly suited his purposes. Now he enjoyed perfect freedom of action. And it should be noted that the breach in the Groupement coincided suspiciously with the resumption of discussions between Krassin, the Russian envoy in London, and Deterding and Sir Basil Zaharov,[6] Leslie Urquhart looking on. But in November the negotiations were shattered.

The Groupement and the Inter-Allied Committee continued to exist side by side. The members of the latter retained their membership in the former. But the Groupement was a mere shadow of its original self; it had become an appendage of the Royal Dutch-Shell without significance or special function. It represented the Deterding organisation and the large Rus-

---

[6] Sir Basil Zaharov, regarded as one of the richest men in the world, is a Greek of French citizenship, born in Russia and bearing a British title.

sian companies into the control of which Sir Henri had bought or manipulated himself. The Deterding bloc convened meetings of the Groupement without even inviting the Franco-Belgians, and then acted upon the resolutions which these meetings had unanimously adopted.[7] A striking example of these tactics was Deterding's attempt to expel from the Groupement the British Spies Petroleum Co. and the Belgian Akverdov and Co. (Petroles de Grosnyi) because they refused to bow without protest to his dictatorship. This attempt soon led to the withdrawal from the Groupement of all the members of the Inter-Allied Committee, thus leaving in the Groupement only the Royal Dutch, the Nobel interests and the Russians, and elicited from the two above-mentioned companies a letter of unusual interest in that it throws light on the activities of the Shell and proves the incorrigibility of Sir Henri who, as late as 1924, had not abandoned the plan, pressed as consistently by him at Genoa and The Hague, of gaining for the Royal Dutch an all-inclusive concession in the Caucasus. The Spies-Akverdov letter reads as follows:

"January 23, 1924.
"To the President, Groupement International
des Sociétés Naphtières en Russie.

"We obtained information yesterday of a letter by which Mr. Gulbenkian has stated on 8th instant that the members of the Groupement International des Sociétés Naphtières unanimously request that we leave

---

[7] See, for instance, the *Petroleum Times* of February 2, 1924.

the Inter-Allied Committee, or, in the alternative, consider ourselves as being dismissed from the Groupement International.

"While pointing out the irregularity of such a decision taken, if, indeed, it was taken, in our absence and without the knowledge of certain members of the Groupement International, who were not even consulted, and taking into consideration that all decisions of the Committee of the Groupement to be valid must be taken unanimously by a general meeting, we regret, for the following reasons, we consider it impossible to collaborate further in the work of the Groupement International.

"(1) The programme of the Groupement International was defined by three fundamental resolutions adopted by the constitutive meeting. These resolutions have been, and continue to be, violated by certain members of the Groupement, in spite of our formal protestations, which have been inscribed upon the minutes of the Committee. As notable instance, we recall the purchase of oil products from the Soviets by the Royal Dutch-Shell Group and the Nobel Group.

"(2) Sir Henri Deterding was charged in certain limited conditions to be the 'porte parole' of the Groupement International to sound the Soviet government upon the question of the restoration pure and simple of confiscated properties. Sir Henri Deterding promised not to conduct negotiations without consulting his colleagues on the Groupement; he has also promised to report in the shortest delay possible upon the first conversations which he had with the Soviets.

This promise has not been fulfilled, and Sir Henri Deterding has continued his conversations direct or indirect, not for the restoration pure and simple of confiscated properties to their legitimate proprietors, but for the constitution of a holding company which would be controlled by his group, and this in allowing incorrect statements to be published that a mandate to this effect has been given to him by the Groupement International.

"(3) At the meeting of the Groupement held on October 25th last, Sir Henri Deterding being absent, delegated Mr. Gulbenkian to report upon the conversations with the Soviet. In reply to questions asked by us, Mr. Gulbenkian categorically stated that the Royal Dutch-Shell has not the intention to constitute a holding company, and that this question has not been raised with the Soviets. This declaration, which was drawn up at the meeting on our demand for inclusion in the procès-verbal, was later suppressed by Mr. Gulbenkian, and the protest raised by us remains without result. In consequence, therefore, of the bad faith of certain members the constitutive resolutions of the Groupement have been violated in the spirit and in the letter. We desire, therefore, to declare formally that we have no further confidence in the present composition of the Groupement, which has lost in our eyes all reason for its existence.

"Taking note that all principles of right and equity are ignored by certain members of the Groupement, and that instead of protecting the interests and rights of oil industrialists who have united for mutual protection, the Groupement itself makes no protest against violations and infractions committed against the said rights, we beg to retire from the Groupement International, reserving our liberty of action for the future."

Soon after this blow, the Groupement sank into oblivion without anybody so much as even taking notice of the event. The Comite Interallie continued a sort of moribund existence. 'Tis said that it meets now and then in Paris. Russians are excluded. The French and the Belgians are more or less faithful to it, but of the British only Messrs. Tweed and Trew attend, and that irregularly. It accomplishes nothing, and can, under the circumstances, accomplish nothing more than the Association of British Creditors of Russia and the corresponding organisation in France, both of which have been attempting to prevent bids for concessions being made to the Soviets, and to bar the influx of "stolen" Soviet oil into their own countries. Yet despite their efforts, Russian petroleum exports continue to increase.

CHAPTER V

STANDARD OIL BACKS RUSSIAN RECOGNITION

Mr. Leslie Urquhart was one of the best and biggest industrialists who operated in Russia before the revolution. Half of his life had been spent in the oil industry of Russia and later he ran what was probably the largest mining enterprise in the Czar's empire. He knew Russia, its language and its people. On May 10, 1922, he wrote as follows in the London *Financial Times*:

"1. The Russian oil-fields are not in a position to export any oil abroad.

"2. To restore production even to the low level of 1917 five years of leeway in the drilling of new wells will have to be made up.

"3. This will require an outlay which cannot, I think, be put at less than £20,000,000 in the aggregate, apart from the heavy expenditure required to reinstate the properties in their former working conditions.

"4. Even if the 1917 level of production is reached, the improvement in Russian transport and industry will absorb the entire yield. For many years to come Russia will be an importer and not an exporter of oil."

"In the main," says the London weekly *Oil News*, which quotes the above in its issue of May 13th, "these are the views which *Oil News* has been impressing upon the public." [1] But alas, prophets on Soviet Russia have made a miserable showing, and even Mr. Urquhart, whose pronouncements one might have expected to be authoritative, permitted the wish to be father to his thoughts. Or perhaps he was reckoning only in terms of pounds sterling, machines and drills, and not in terms of national vitality released by the revolution, of the devotion, energy, persistence, enthusiasm and of other non-businesslike factors by means of which the Bolsheviks upset the calculations of the finest hard-headed experts.

Certain it is that history has proven Mr. Urquhart decidedly in the wrong. For the country which, for many years after 1922, would, as he said, "be an importer and not an exporter of oil", has from that day to this, imported not a single ton, barrel, or pound of oil. Instead it *exported* (in round figures) 330,000 tons in the fiscal year 1922–23, 771,000 tons in the fiscal year 1923–24 (exclusive of China and Persia), 1,360,000 tons in the fiscal year 1924–25.

Any impartial person must judge this record an exceptional achievement, for it was made without the foreign assistance and capital on which practically

[1] Soon after this solemn declaration the *Oil News* repented, and the issue of October 25, 1924, contains this passage:

"Pursuing the line of thought we have followed for some year or two past [?], which has so far been justified by events, we think it of advantage to make a remark or two upon the inevitable expansion of the Russian oil industry. . . . The Russian export trade has grown during the past twelve months quite beyond the expectation of those who might have been expected to be able to make the best forecast of it. . . . One by one the various countries of Europe are becoming important customers of Russia."

the entire Russian petroleum industry was dependent before the revolution, and against the bitter opposition of many of the governments and—at one time or another—of almost all the important oil trusts of the world.

The import of Russian oil products has met with greatest opposition in England and France. Here the former owners of Russian petroleum properties have done their utmost to prevent the marketing of "stolen" liquid by arrant "thieves". Nevertheless England is the best customer of the Naphtha Syndicate, and France does not fall far behind. In 1924–25, for instance, the British Empire—the system which should be most interested in obstructing the economic rehabilitation of Russia because it is probably by means of forces emanating from Russia that that system will be shattered—bought 34,000,000 [2] of the 81,000,-000 poods which the Soviet oil syndicate sold to foreign countries. Second place is held by Italy with 14,998,000 poods, and third by Germany with 10,964,-000 poods. France follows with 8,506,000 poods. The United States, for obvious reasons, is not in the list— but the Russians say it will be before many years have elapsed.

Soviet oil, notwithstanding all obstacles, is playing an increasingly important rôle in the industry and commerce of European and Near Eastern nations. Ac-

[2] These were divided as follows:
20,285,000 poods to the United Kingdom.
11,157,000   "   " Egypt.
1,696,000   "   " India, and
908,000   "   " Malta for the British Fleet.

cording to official Russian data, the Naphtha Syndicate supplied:

Germany with 9.6% of her oil imports in 1923–24, and 24.8% in 1924–25.

France with 4.3% of her oil imports in 1923–24, and 9.9% in 1924–25.

Italy with 7.7% of her oil imports in 1923–24, and 40.8% in 1924–25.

Turkey with 28.6% of her oil imports in 1923–24, and 46.7% in 1924–25.

Jugo-Slavia with 0.0% of her oil imports in 1923–24, and 13.8% in 1924–25.

Egypt with 25.0% of her oil imports in 1923–24, and 47.3% in 1924–25.

England with 3.8% of her oil imports in 1923–24, and 5.8% in 1924–25.

These comparative percentages present a clear picture of the progress made by Soviet petroleum in the course of twelve months, but it requires the absolute tonnage figures to complete the impression. These are, in English tons:

	1923–24	*1924–25*
Germany	69,100	175,500
France	56,600	137,300
Italy	41,900	241,840
Turkey	16,200	31,800
Jugo-Slavia	0	8,300
Egypt	75,000	180,400
England	180,200	321,600

Incongruous though it may seem, it is nevertheless a fact that the Naphtha Syndicate of the Bolshevik state now supplies oil for the navies of four capitalistic Powers: Great Britain, France, Italy and Greece. On March 24, 1925, an agreement was signed in Moscow by G. Lomov, the president of the Naphtha Syndicate, and J. Herbette, the French ambassador, for the delivery to the French Ministry of Marine of 75,000 tons of fuel oil before the end of the year.[3] After an interview between Lomov and Mussolini late in 1924 a similar arrangement was made for the Italian fleet. Italy is, by all indications, one of Russia's best prospective oil customers. During 1925, all of Italy's fuel oil came from the Caucasus. "Italian industry," says the London *Oil News* of December 13, 1924, "is likely to require next year about 120,000 tons of fuel oil; and we stated in last week's *Oil News* that an Italian consortium has contracted with the Russian Naphtha Syndicate for the supply of that quantity during the twelve months." On April 18, 1925, the same publication announced that a contract had been signed for the delivery of 240,000 tons of various petrol products

---

[3] It was to have been expected that the French holders of Russian oil paper would object to this deal. On April 9th, according to the London *Petroleum Times,* the Franco-Belgian Syndicate sent a letter of protest to the Quai D'Orsay, which said that "the purchase of petroleum products from the Soviets is a violation of the resolution adopted both at Genoa and The Hague, and the French government has thus injured the legitimate interests of the petroleum companies having interests in Russia, from whose wells the Soviets are obtaining the products which they are selling to France."

"Attention is also drawn [in the letter] to the fact that it was the French decision at Genoa which prevented the foreign trusts getting possession of the Russian oil-fields."

during 1926. The Naphtha Syndicate has struck the Anglo-Persian Company a heavy blow on the Italian market and there are cautious observers who venture the prophecy that before long this company as well as the Standard Oil will be entirely eliminated. Similarly rapid progress is registered in Turkey where, as in England, the Naphtha Syndicate is erecting its own tanks and establishing its own retail selling apparatus. Here too the Soviets are faced by the stubborn competition of the Standard Oil which, in many cases, has cut prices in an unsuccessful attempt to destroy the Red intruder. In Bulgaria, which is a neighbour of oil-producing Roumania, Russia is driving out Roumanian oil, and the Roumanian Commercial Attaché in Sofia reports to his government that "Russian products are obtaining an introduction and securing the position hitherto held by Roumanian commodities. The Soviet interests are making all possible efforts to improve their lamp oil, oils, etc. The Bulgarians, familiar with Russian lamp oil, begin to appreciate it and all the more so because it is cheaper and of superior quality." [4] This from a Roumanian official. Even in Egypt, one of the bulwarks of the British Empire, the oil of Caucasus is causing considerable annoyance to the powerful British trusts. For no one any more disputes that in the Mediterranean basin Russian oil is practically invincible.

Limited in volume though Russia's exports be, they have from time to time, and especially in England and France, aroused the ire and provoked the protestations

[4] London *Oil News*, December 26, 1925.

of former owners of oil properties in the Caucasus. But since these periodic outbursts were more often than not inspired by oil companies whose business was damaged by the penetration of Soviet petroleum into markets in which they were interested, the protests inevitably became fewer as, one by one, most of these companies themselves became customers of the Naphtha Syndicate. But in Great Britain, in the latter half of 1925, the crusade against Russian oil suddenly flared up with more than usual vigor.

The crusade was not conducted by petroleum firms —not directly, at least. It was managed by the Association of British Creditors of Russia. There are people who suggest that this association is a mere tool of the Royal Dutch-Shell and does its bidding just as it did the bidding of Leslie Urquhart and acted as a mouthpiece for the former Russian mining interests in the early part of its existence when the organisation's offices were located in Urquhart's office. There are people who go so far as to suggest that the latest campaign against the sale in England of Soviet petroleum was set in motion with a sum of money placed at the disposal of the association by a member of Deterding's family. Mr. Stafford Talbot, himself a British creditor, and editor of the *British-Russian Gazette and Trade Outlook*, once remarked to me that "oil shouts loudly in the name of the British creditors", and it is certainly remarkable that the chairman of the association is R. R. Tweed, the president of the Baku Consolidated Oil-fields, Ltd., the vice-chairmen are Percy R. Clark, managing director of the Baku Wire

Rope Cable Co., and H. Gwynne Trew, managing director of the Spies Petroleum Co., while the secretary is F. H. Coe, an employee of the Baku Consolidated.

The Association of British Creditors of Russia (ABC of Russia) worked most energetically to frustrate the settlement between Russia and Britain in 1924 which MacDonald, the then premier, and Rakovsky, the then Soviet ambassador in London, had arrived at. And, with the similarly hostile forces which it easily mobilised around its banner, it succeeded. In the press and in Parliament it continues the agitation against an arrangement with Moscow to this very day.

The ABC's campaign against the sale of Soviet oil in the autumn of 1925 was, in a way, part of the general scheme of obstructing Anglo-Russian trade and filling the air with anti-Soviet propaganda. But it was more than that. Measured by the amount of space given by the newspapers and by the volume of reading matter distributed to the public, the campaign was eminently successful. Yet, from another point of view, it perhaps did the association more harm than good in that it revealed the true oleous face and predominant oil interests of the Creditors' organisation.

The campaign under discussion was aimed at the Russian Oil Products, Ltd., a Russian company which commenced its activities in England in August, 1924. It was against this company that the Creditors' Association fired its Orange Pamphlet entitled *Justice or Plunder; The Facts about Soviet Confiscation and Dishonesty; Soviet Oil Scandal.* The Russian Oil Products (ROP), we are told in a foreword signed by Messrs. Tweed and Trew, "is endeavouring to sell the stolen goods in this country." Having taken the oil-fields, the Soviet government was actually trying to sell the products of these oil-fields to their former owners or fellow nationals.

The pamphlet closed with a demand that the British government appoint a committee to amend the Anglo-Russian Trade Agreement of 1921 under the terms of which the ROP operates in the United Kingdom, and failure on the part of the Soviets to acquiesce to the proposed amendments was "to be considered as reasonable grounds for the immediate termination of the existing agreement." In other words—a complete interruption of relations with Russia.

Soon after the publication of the anti-ROP brochure, questions were on two occasions put in the House of Commons which raised the same objections as did the pamphlet and which repeated its recommendations with regard to the Anglo-Russian Trade Agreement. Meanwhile, the press printed a number of letters on the subject. Sir N. Grattan Doyle, M.P., protested against allowing the competition of Russian oil. Mr. Tweed wrote in to say that Sir Grattan had performed a public service by so doing, and then proceeded to argue the points of confiscation and retaliation. Sir Henri Deterding addressed the editor of the *Times* and gave facts purporting to show that "oil stocks belonging to and paid for by British and other companies were seized and exported and the proceeds cashed by the Soviet government." "Sir Grattan," Deterding concluded, "in asking whether it is decent to allow such competition, might have used stronger words had he known the above."

Yet Sir Henri had himself purchased close to half a million tons of "stolen" Soviet oil between 1921 and 1925. Why was he protesting now? Why had there been no campaign when the Shell was an eager buyer of Russian petroleum?

The campaign against the ROP reached its height in November. During the following month I was fortunate enough to be received by Messrs. Tweed and Trew. My impression after several conversations was definitely that they were anxious to avoid any reference to their conflicts with and opposition to Deterding during the days of Genoa, The Hague, the Groupement and the Inter-Allied Committee. The moving spirits of the Creditors' Association and Sir Henri seemed to have buried the hatchet and identified the cause of the former with the interests of the latter.

When the agitation was at its height, the London *Oil News* refused to accept further advertisements of the ROP, and boasted on November 7th that "we have evidence that all important oil marketing concerns except one (and we leave our readers to guess which one that is) have expressed directly or indirectly approval of our action." This reader guesses that the one exception was the Standard Oil, or rather its British branch, the Anglo-American Oil Co., and he further suggests that one of the moving forces of the campaign was the desire of the Shell to embarrass the Standard in its negotiations to buy large quantities of "stolen" Russian products.

No doubt a motive behind the association's agitation was the fact that the ROP is a company whose specific and only purpose it is to retail oil in the United Kingdom. The ROP has its own reservoirs in Cardiff and Bristol, and its own selling apparatus, and what is more, it retails benzine, kerosene and other products at between one and three pennies below the market price of other oil-selling agencies in Great Britain. These agencies, which have an agreement with regard to price levels, are naturally annoyed by the undercutting of the young Russian upstart. As long as the Royal Dutch was able to purchase Soviet petroleum wholesale, its directors chose to forget that it was "stolen". The introduction of the Caucasian product upon the retail market, however, was the signal for a general attack. In this connection it must be remarked that according to official figures furnished by the British Customs there were imported during the first nine months of 1925 considerably over 78 million gallons of Russian petroleum products of which only 13,473,-000 gallons were consigned to the ROP and the remainder to mammoth wholesalers, one of which was the Shell.

But the campaign against the ROP synchronised with important conversations between the Naphtha Syndicate and the Anglo-American, and in view of Sir Henri Deterding's rather clumsy effort in the *Times* and of another similarly ineffective effort in the *Morning Post* of June 5, 1925, as well as of circumstances and impressions mentioned above, we cannot but suppose that the crusade launched by the Association of British

Creditors of Russia was not unrelated to the world-wide and ancient rivalry between the Royal Dutch-Shell and the Standard Oil.[5]

It should be borne in mind, of course, that the total of Russia's exports, compared with the world's oil trade, is small though significant. Nevertheless, Soviet oil exports last year exceeded the norm of pre-war years [6] when they were heavily financed from abroad and assisted by the encouragement and good-will of all. Despite a boycott supported by governments, notwithstanding virulent campaigns by angry creditors against the purchase of "stolen" wares, and undeterred by repeated questions in the House of Commons and the Chamber of Deputies so framed as to serve the purposes of anti-Soviet-oil propaganda, Russian petroleum continues to find an ever-growing foreign market.

[5] The anti-ROP campaign was not the first instance of special bias against the Standard on the part of the British Creditors. In February, 1925, when the Anglo-American purchased 20,000 tons of Soviet petrol and obtained an option for 500,000 tons more, the Association immediately circulated a protest on the ground that the oil came from stolen and confiscated properties. But this Association, remarked the *Oil News* of March 7th, did not protest against British purchases of Russian oil. "That being so," continues the weekly, "why should hostility be saved up for the Anglo-American which has at all events not done its deal in secret," as the Shell had done, the editor meant to add. "We imagine," the paper proceeds, "that should the official announcement be confirmed [it was], the transaction is an unwelcome one for the Royal Dutch and Shell group."

We wonder whether it was not precisely because the purchase was unsavory to Deterding's organisation that the Creditors' Association issued its protest, and whether it is not because the larger purchase of Soviet oil now contemplated by the Anglo-American (or the Standard Oil) would be even more unsavoury to Sir Henri that the Creditors went to the length of a broadside of protests against the ROP.

[6] In 1913 Russia exported 57,800,000 poods of oil; in 1924-25 81,000,000 poods.

Three elements contribute to this success: (1) the superior quality of Russian oil; (2) the proximity of the Caucasus to European markets; (3) the scarcity of oil resources in Europe.

(1) I have heard non-Russian former owners as well as Russians state that the product of Baku was the best in the world. This may be an exaggeration dictated by sentiment in the one case and policy in the other. But the quality is certainly very excellent. Grosni furnished a liquid of unusually high paraffin content, while Emba petroleum is a fine foundation for rich machine and lubricating oils. To be sure, the Russian refining industry is backward. The varieties of oil manufactured by the Baku plants are very few; the processes used in the Caucasus for "cracking" and extracting benzine are not up-to-date; much goes to waste and many by-products are not utilised. Nevertheless there has been improvement all along the line. The Baku fields have been partly electrified—"Americanised", the Russians say. Equipment for "cracking" and refining has been brought from the United States, and in especially great quantities since the visit to America of Serebrovsky, the head of the Azerbaijan Oil Trust. The rotary system of drilling has become widespread and is forcing out the more primitive methods. Inevitably, Russia will lag behind in this respect for a number of years, but the realisation is general that modernisation is imperative, and every effort is being made to increase efficiency, productivity, quality and variety.

(2) With respect to the Near East and all the

countries in the Mediterranean basin, Russia undoubtedly has the handicap of transport on Persian oil, on the oil brought by the Shell from the East Indies and Burma, and on the Royal Dutch and Standard Oil which must carry from Mexico, South America, or from western United States. The Caucasus is within short and cheap distance by water of Turkey, Egypt, the Balkans, Italy and France. Since the freight charge in oil is an important item of cost, the Soviet Naphtha Syndicate has an undeniable advantage.

In regard to Central Europe and the Baltic countries to which Russia can and does deliver petrol by rail, she has a distinct lead on the Anglo-Persian whose centre of production is far away on the Persian Gulf, as well as on the companies drawing their "gas" from Venezuela or Mexico or the islands of the Pacific, and, finally, if the intention of some Soviet leaders to exploit the resources of Sakhalien side by side with the Japanese ever materialises, Russia will become a serious competitor of the Standard Oil and Royal Dutch in that vast, and potentially vaster, oil market which China represents. We must not, however, lose sight of the fact that the powerful capitalist oil trusts have well-functioning distribution systems in lands where the Naphtha Syndicate is only beginning to gain a foothold; that, moreover, Russia has few tankers and a small quantity of tank cars. These circumstances will seriously retard the advances which Soviet oil can make in foreign markets. But when all is said, they are temporary. The money which the sale of Caucasian oil abroad is bringing into the Moscow ex-

chequer is being used to remove the difficulties, and
should ultimately succeed in reducing their harm to a
minimum. Geography, on the other hand, is immutable,
and here the Soviets benefit much by the position of
the Russian oil-fields with respect to the great industrial countries of Europe.

(3) But the greatest advantage is, obviously, the
last: outside of Russia there is little oil in Europe.
European production is thus itemised by the *Statesman's Year Book* of 1925:

	1922	*1923*	*1924*
	(In metric tons)		
Russia	3,973,510	5,435,000	6,653,000
Roumania ..	1,365,765	1,512,000	1,811,600
Poland	732,482	733,000	670,000
France	60,000	57,000	56,600
Germany ...	34,967	44,000	45,700

Clearly, Russia outranks them all. What Germany
and France produce is even less than the drop in the
proverbial bucket. Poland's wells are fast deteriorating, and while Roumanian production has been rising
in recent years, the yield of the country is actually and
potentially so far below that of the Russian Union, and
so infinitesimal in comparison with Europe's needs, that
its rôle is necessarily limited though, for the present,
important.

The oil magnates of the world are not oblivious to
the value and significance of the Russian oil deposits.
Of this the efforts of the Royal Dutch, of the Standard,

and of Sinclair to acquire controlling interests in them is sufficient testimony. Latterly, however, the efforts of the petrol companies have been concentrated, at least with respect to the Caucasus, not so much on concessions, but on the purchase of large quantities of Soviet oil products. During 1923, and the first half of 1924, the Standard Oil permitted the Shell combine complete freedom in this field. But in the summer of 1924, it is said, a Paris conference between Standard and Shell representatives agreed that the situation was to be reversed, on condition, however, the Standard would share its purchases of Russian oil with the Shell if the latter so desired. The fact is that just at this time the American trust commenced buying from the Moscow Naphtha Syndicate while the Royal Dutch-Shell interrupted its dealings with it, and that in March, 1925, a large shipment of oil bought by the Standard at Batum was consigned directly to the Asiatic Petroleum Company, a Shell subsidiary.[7]

[7] This touches upon the ever-intriguing and much-mooted question of the relations between the Standard Oil and the Royal Dutch-Shell combine. How many times has it been rumoured that they have amalgamated? How often has it been stated in the press that they have merged their interests? The definite piece of cooperation referred to here seems to support the view that these two international oil mammoths have actually joined hands. Such an interpretation would be incorrect. The point is that generalisations are impossible on this subject. The Standard Oil and Royal Dutch-Shell cooperate in separate fields of endeavour or on individual transactions whenever it suits their purpose to do so. They may, for instance, agree on maintaining a certain level of prices in certain countries. But outside of these limits they remain sharp competitors. This must be especially true in the United States and Mexico where, as the American supply decreases, the presence of the Royal Dutch-Shell will be more and more resented by its most powerful rival.

The Standard Oil now became a regular customer of the Russians, and between August, 1924, and April, 1925, purchased approximately 290,000 tons of kerosene and benzine. These transactions, however, were mere preliminaries to a much more ambitious plan of the Standard Oil's. The House of Rockefeller proposed nothing less than its purchase of the entire production of all the Russian oil-fields for a period of from three to five years. Anyone familiar with Bolshevik policy and tactics would have realised beforehand that such an offer would be refused, for the Communists are unalterably averse to placing themselves at the mercy of a single company or country unless a catastrophic economic crisis compelled them to do so. In 1922 Russia was stricken by famine; the industrial life of the land was chaotic; the government was in severe financial straits. Then an all-inclusive concession to the Royal Dutch was conceivable. But in 1925, when economic rehabilitation was proceeding at a fast pace and when financial contacts had been established with Europe and America, when, moreover, oil products were finding an ever-readier market in Europe, there was no consideration which could force the Soviets to yield up so vast an asset as their petroleum exports to a single trust, especially in view of the fact that the Standard had been extremely hostile and that the United States had not established relations with the Russian government.

The Bolsheviks realised from the start that the good-will of the Standard Oil, which would be forthcoming upon an arrangement between it and the Russians, would do much to pave the way to a resumption of relations between the two countries. Early in the spring of 1925 I was discussing Russo-American relations in Moscow with Chicherin, and he hinted, rather mysteriously, that these would possibly improve in the event of a change of attitude of the Standard Oil, which then seemed impending.[8] Months later a high official of the Russian Naphtha Syndicate admitted to me that the political factor was a point in favour of the Standard Oil in any negotiations with the Syndicate. Nevertheless, not even the consideration of American recognition could, at this late stage in Russia's economic recovery, incline Moscow to grant the Standard Oil a monopoly of oil exports over a period of years. This certainly was the consensus of opinion in high Soviet circles in 1925 when the proposal was first advanced by the Americans, and accordingly Premier Rykov frankly stated in an interview that no such offer was acceptable.

The Soviet refusal, however, did not put a stop to negotiations. Both parties are eager for an agreement, the Americans perhaps more so than the Russians. But in view of the importance and far-reach-

[8] With regard to the relationship between oil and America's foreign policy, Davenport and Cooke in their *Oil Trusts and Anglo-American Relations*, write: "In point of fact, a national interest in or anxiety about the supply of oil was all that was needed to give the United States a foreign policy in oil identical with the policy of the Standard Oil. That, as we have seen, emerged after the Armistice from natural mercantile ambitions. The Secretary of State and the President of the Standard Oil were soon to be pulling together with a will!"

"As Sir W. Tyrell (the permanent head of the British Foreign Office) remarked, Washington began to think, talk and write like Standard Oil officials."

ing character of any settlement, in view, moreover, of the political considerations involved, neither of the parties is inclined to be precipitate. More often than not, however, the initiative has been on the part of the Americans. The Standard Oil, of course, can manage without Russian oil this year and next, and the year after as well, probably. Yet long-visioned directors are looking to 1930 and to the critical decade in the oil industry which it will introduce. It is not necessary to be alarmist, for even a dispassionate judgment brings one to the same conclusion: before many years will have elapsed the United States must lose its foreign oil market unless new sources of supply outside the Western Hemisphere are acquired by American petroleum interests.

The United States is at present importing oil to satisfy its own demand. Until 1920 the United States was exporting more oil than she was importing. Since then she has been exporting only at the expense of her imports. In 1921 the United States exported 2,712,000,000 gallons and in 1922 3,012,000,000 gallons less than she imported, while in 1923, imports exceeded exports by 1,099,000,000 gallons despite the fact that during that year her production rose by more than 7,000,000,000 gallons. (In 1924 United States production declined.)

The deduction is phrased for us by no less eminent an authority than the National City Bank of New York, which rumour has it, is not unrelated to the Standard Oil interests. In the June, 1925, monthly letter of the bank, we read: "There is no question, however, that in the future the world supply of crude oil must be obtained in larger part from countries other than the United States."

It is not for nothing that the Standard Oil has been striking out towards North Persia, Mosul and Palestine, and bidding for concessions in Africa and the Dutch East Indies. For unless the Rockefeller firm soon finds supplementary resources in Eurasia its hold on the markets of the Eastern Hemisphere is destined to disappear in the next few years. More than this. If Henry Ford, the General Motors Company and their competitors continue to turn out oil-consumers in the millions as they have been doing—and there is no reason why they should stop—if, furthermore, more and more ships take to burning oil and an increasing number of Diesel engines enter industry, it is not impossible that the United States will, within the next decade, become dependent on Russian oil. To make a definite prophecy would of course be foolhardy. Some unknown resources may be discovered. Although in the last years many new fields and wells in the United States and Mexico have come into operation still consumption is greater than production. Government departments and oil men are evidencing increasing alarm—and justly so.

Considerations such as these actuated the Standard Oil in making its offer to the Soviet Naphtha Syndicate to buy the entire Russian yield over a period of years. When this offer was rejected, negotiations were entered into with a view to arriving at a compromise arrangement. The Bolsheviks proposed to sell the

Standard fifty per cent. of their production.   They were even prepared to retire from certain markets—Germany, the Scandinavian countries, Belgium, etc. But they wished to reserve for themselves the right to sell oil in the Mediterranean basin from which the Russians are anxious to exclude British competition and especially in Turkey where economic interests are probably not unmixed with political considerations.

This proposal was, generally speaking, more or less acceptable to the Standard Oil.   But the Standard made the proviso that the Naphtha Syndicate must sell petroleum products to it at a price lower than that which would be paid by the purchasers of the fifty per cent. not sold to the American trust, this in order to enable the Standard to compensate some of the former proprietors whose fields had been appropriated by the Soviets.

The Russian negotiators rejected the proviso.   The Standard agent offered to supply the Moscow Syndicate with a credit of $25,000,000 and to build a pipeline from the important oil-field of Grosni to the city of Tuapse on the Black Sea.   But the Bolsheviks were adamant and as a result the conversations broke off.

Neither party, however, despaired of reaching an agreement.   In October, 1925, the Standard Oil again intimated that it was anxious to renew pourparlers with the Soviet Naphtha Syndicate, and preliminary conversations commenced in London.   It soon appeared that the councils of the Standard Oil as well as of the Syndicate were divided on some of the fundamental questions involved. The Vacuum Oil Co., a subsidiary of the Standard Oil, which does considerable business in Egypt and the Near East generally, was enthusiastically in favour of buying Russian oil. The Standard Oil Company of New York (Socony), had no objections to doing so. But the Standard Oil of New Jersey (Soconej) was rather cold to the proposition.

The explanation of these varying attitudes is not far to seek. Vacuum Oil conducts a heavy business in the Mediterranean basin and bears much of the brunt of Soviet competition. Socony is interested in the Turkish and Bulgarian markets which it cannot long hold without the assistance of shipments from the Caucasus. Whether or no one shares this opinion depends on one's view of the future of the American oil industry. With regard to petroleum resources in the United States, American oil men are divided. There are those who have a pessimistic outlook and believe the available reserves will be exhausted within the lifetime of our generation. The Federal Oil Conservation Board appointed by President Coolidge in 1925 mirrors this view. It is also concurred in by Secretary of Commerce Herbert Hoover, who, as early as December 10, 1922, in a report of the Department of Commerce, anticipated the depletion of the underground oil supplies of his country and advised his fellow nationals to seek concessions in foreign lands.

Contrariwise, a large section of American oil opinion is more optimistic. It holds that the reserves amount to twenty-six billion barrels and not to between five and six billion as the Federal Oil Conservation Board

would have it. The convictions of this group are
set forth in a volume report of American Petroleum
Institute entitled *American Petroleum—Supply and
Demand.* Now Mr. Teagle, the chairman of the Board
of Directors of the Soconej is in complete agreement
with the optimists. The November 28, 1925, issue of
the *Saturday Evening Post* published an article on
"Tomorrow's Gasoline" by W. C. Teagle, in which the
writer adduces innumerable facts to allay the fears of
those who may be fretting over the likelihood of an
impending "oil famine". Nevertheless, even this
prophet of a rosy future is not altogether blind to the
possibilities of unfavourable developments in the American supply, and in the article whose obvious purpose
is to dispel any thoughts which may disturb the com-
placency of his millions of Babbit readers, he is forced
to contemplate such an eventuality. He says: "The
extension of American activities in foreign petroleum
fields—which has been accomplished in the face of all
the difficulties I have enumerated—has been comparatively recent. It has, however, been fruitful, as evi-
denced by the fact that in 1924 more than 40 per
cent. of all crude production outside the United States
was obtained by companies directly or indirectly
American owned. There arises a natural conjecture
as to the outcome should the gradual decline of present producing fields in this country fail to be supplemented by new petroleum areas and by yields from
deeper sands in established fields. The location of
the chief sources of supply would then be transferred
to other countries, and the question has sometimes been

asked whether existing companies could face such a revolutionary readjustment. Though the contingency is remote, it may be said that the machinery of the industry is of a character which could speedily adjust itself to the new conditions."

In Mr. Teagle's opinion, then, the possibility exists but the "contingency is remote". It is this belief, on which, incidentally, some of his closest associates differ with him, that probably explains part of the Soconej's lukewarmness to purchases of Soviet oil.

But by far the most potent factor in the Soconej's attitude is the fear of the Shell and the influence of Sir Henri Deterding. Sir Henry is intent on preventing a deal between the Russians and the Standard. For what other reason did he consent to make himself the laughing stock of his own fellow directors by writing a letter to the London *Morning Post* in which he prophesied the fall of the Soviet government before the end of 1926? Deterding knows full well, unless he is completely out of his wits, that there is not the slightest indication of any weakening of Bolshevik power in Russia. Yet many otherwise intelligent people are prepared to credit even the silliest canard about Soviet Russia, and Deterding, understanding how to exploit this circumstance as well as the deplorable paucity of reliable information in America on Russia, has tried through the columns of the Tory *Post*, and through other channels as well, to emphasise the "folly" of concluding an important contract with a government whose collapse is imminent. His letter to the *Post* cannot be accepted as a literary exercise.

Nor was it a vent for his anti-Bolshevism. He has none in business. The letter and the prediction it contained are a transparent attempt to terrify the Standard Oil of New Jersey with which Sir Henri has close dealings. The Soconej operates in France, Italy, Germany, Scandinavia and other countries which are large consumers of petrol. Here it competes with the Royal Dutch-Shell. But what is officially styled "competition" is in reality cooperation, for instead of struggling against one another and thus reducing their profits to a minimum, the two giants of the oil world "combine", so to speak, and agree to a common market price. Deterding, accordingly, has a powerful weapon against the Standard. Only recently he threatened a price war with the Vacuum Oil if it sold Soviet petroleum in Egypt. The Vacuum is ready to defy him—very likely because it does not suppose that the Shell would throw down the gauntlet to the Standard for the sake of the Egyptian market. But Mr. Teagle has reason to fear that Deterding would go to such lengths if his business in all the important countries of Europe were imperilled by an understanding between the Soconej and the Russians. This, more than any speculation on the future of the American industry, and far more than any question of morals, was at the bottom of Teagle's disinclination to deal with the Syndicate. This, too, explains the Soconej's concern about "stolen" oil.

In January, 1926, Standard officials favourable to an agreement with the Bolsheviks made a determined effort to establish a "United Front" of Standard Oil interests. A representative of the Anglo-American Oil Company, who possesses considerable knowledge of Russian trade in Europe, was sent to New York to convince those Standard leaders who needed convincing that now was the time to buy as much Soviet petroleum as possible. He had no difficulty in winning the support of the Vacuum Oil and the Socony. But Mr. Teagle was the strategic fort which had to be taken, and this fort was surrounded by a moat ostensibly named "morality". Apparently, however, Mr. Teagle feared that his knowledge of the oil business was greater than his grasp of moral principles. He accordingly summoned for consultation no less an authority on the subject than Charles Evans Hughes, ex-Secretary of State. This pillar of society met with several Standard directors and with the delegates of the Anglo-American to deliberate on whether it was moral and ethical to enter into negotiations for the purchase of "stolen" oil. Several persons present at that meeting submitted that in practice, if not in theory, this knotty problem had already been solved, for the Standard had theretofore bought many tens of thousands of tons of this very tainted petroleum, and that the Shell has bought even more. It was pointed out further that the United States was doing an increasing amount of business with Soviet Russia and that Russian Communists who came to place orders in America were readily granted visas by the State Department even though Communists who had no business to offer were refused permission to enter the country. "Business is business" more or less epitomises the arguments of those participants in the conference who advised a transaction with the Soviet Naphtha Syndicate.

Rumour has it that even the Olympic morals of the redoubtable Hughes were shaken by this contention, and that he acknowledged himself persuaded. Be that as it may, it does appear that the Standard directors and even Mr. Teagle looked upon the proposition of purchasing Russian oil in a more friendly light after this meeting, and that the Anglo-American delegate returned to London authorised to truck with the Bolsheviks and to buy their oil—all of it if the Syndicate proved willing. More than this. *The startling fact has now been revealed that the Soconej would even accept a concession for the Emba oil-field.* Moscow would prefer not to part with Emba, but owing to the necessity of considerable capital investments to raise the productivity of the field, in view, furthermore, of the lack of transportation facilities serving Emba, there is an inclination on the part of certain Soviet political circles not to repel a serious bid for a concession to Emba, and I believe I am right in saying that an offer from the Standard Oil would receive more sympathetic consideration than that of any other organisation, provided always, of course, that the American government refrains from anti-Soviet activity and agitation.

On the other hand, Moscow appears to be divided into two camps with regard to selling large quantities of oil to the Standard Oil subsidiaries. The one body of opinion feels that Soviet oil exports are finding an ever larger market without great difficulty. The Syndicate is having, and should in the near future have, no trouble in disposing of all the exportable surpluses of the Russian oil industry. Unless, therefore, the Standard Oil is prepared to advance appreciable sums for the purpose of raising the production of the Russian oil-fields, there is no great advantage to the Russians in entering into an ambitious agreement for Soviet oil sales to the Standard Oil. If in consequence of financial investment by the Rockefeller trust or as a result of large-size credits made available to the Bolsheviks through the good offices of the Standard, many million poods are added to Russia's annual petroleum output, the Standard will be given first claim on this excess yield. Should the curve of production in the Caucasus and elsewhere, however, rise with the same or even somewhat greater degree of steepness than it has in the last two years, it serves no important purpose for the Bolsheviks to bind themselves by an inclusive contract with the Standard. This is the argument of one school of thought.

The other contends that it requires an extensive and costly machinery of distribution to sell large quantities of oil abroad at a profit. With many of the governments of the world and many of the oil companies hostile to the Bolsheviks there is no guarantee that a selling apparatus, once established in a country, will be permitted to function without let or hindrance. Indeed, there is even the possibility that its operations will some day be prohibited altogether. In view of these two considerations, the Soviet Naphtha Syndicate cannot afford to retail its oil in foreign countries, especially when the big trusts have now taken to setting up thousands upon thousands of wayside pumping stations. Against such methods the Russians cannot hope to compete at present. It follows that they must dispose of their surpluses through the world petroleum trusts, and one is as good or as bad as the other. Since the Standard will probably be able and prepared to pay a better price than its chief rival, the Royal Dutch-Shell, and since the government of the United States, even without having recognised the Soviet Union, is not inspired by as bitter an antagonism for the Bolsheviks as is Great Britain, there is no reason why the chosen one should not be the Standard Oil Company.

Which of these two contentions will make the firmer imprint on the final policy of the Soviet Naphtha Syndicate depends largely on the details of the Standard Oil's bid.

During the stay of the Anglo-American's representative in New York a projected contract between the Vacuum Oil and the Syndicate was drafted for submission to the Russians as a basis for negotiations. It provided for the sale to the Vacuum Oil of three to four hundred thousand tons of crude oil, gasoline, and kerosene. These were to be sold to the Vacuum Oil in Egypt, Palestine, Syria, Cilicia, Cyprus, Poland, Czecho-Slovakia, Jugo-Slavia, Austria, Hungary, Portugal, and Morocco. The draft agreement specified that any oil which the Soviet Syndicate might wish to sell through channels other than the Vacuum Oil must be sold through the Standard Oil of New York, and the Standard Oil of New Jersey.

For these countries at least, therefore, the Standard combine demanded a monopoly. This is a most unsavoury feature for the Bolsheviks. It is at least as important as the question of price, and was certain to cause difficulties in the negotiations. One can conceive of the Russians agreeing in principle to a modified or restricted monopoly, but they could hardly consent to a monopoly in practice in all the countries enumerated in the Vacuum Oil's draft contract.

The Socony is especially interested in Turkey. For some reason, the Standard attaches a significance to the Turkish market which far transcends its value as a consumer.

On this subject a special correspondent of the Manchester *Guardian Commercial* writes: "From the American point of view, the turnover [in the Turkish oil market] is quite negligible." Observers have remarked that the Standard Oil is paying far more attention to the market in Asiatic Turkey than it deserves, and that it seems prepared to make great sacrifices in other spheres in order to fortify itself in Anatolia even though it is patent that that poor, non-industrial country is hardly worth a small fraction of the effort the Rockefeller trust is putting into it. This circumstance has given rise to a suspicion, which other facts help to confirm, that the Standard wishes to build itself a berth in Turkey more with a view to obtaining an exploiting concession for oil resources in territories now ruled from Angora or in Mosul, should a satisfactory compromise solution of the Mosul boundary dispute be effected between Great Britain and Turkey, than because the Standard directors are interested in selling several additional thousand tons of oil to the Anatolian peasants. Be that as it may, it is a fact that the Socony is bent on maintaining its hold on the Turkish market. Trouble is created by the attitude of the Turkish authorities. On January 25, 1926, the National Assembly at Angora declared the distribution of oil a monopoly of the State; the act to go into effect on March 25th of the same year. But it is not yet certain where the Turkish government will buy its petroleum. Now approximately forty-five per cent. of the oil consumed by Turkey is sold by the Naphtha Syndicate, and about fifty per cent. by the Standard Oil, but every drop of the Standard Oil's fifty per cent. is bought from the Naphtha Syndicate. It follows that Angora would purchase oil either from the Russians or from the Americans. The Turkish consumer knows and is accustomed to the Russian product. Moreover, the Americans are aware that the Kemal régime is on terms of cordial relationship with Moscow. Accordingly, the Standard realises that if it wishes to maintain its hold on the Turkish market—and we have indicated that it most decidedly does so wish—it must effect an understanding with the Soviet Syndicate. The Standard therefore proposes a pooling of interests with the Russians which would take the form of a partnership monopoly allowing for the sale of the Caucasian liquid by the Syndicate as well as the Standard. The Rockefeller negotiations in

Berlin and Paris have been unable to disguise their anxiety to reach such a settlement, and it was abundantly clear to those few who were privileged to watch the course of the preliminary conversations that the Turkish complex was playing an extremely dominating rôle in the Standard-Syndicate conferences. The insistence of the Americans on an economic oil condominium in Turkey with the Russians, however, involves important considerations of Soviet diplomacy, and it is rather doubtful whether Moscow could agree to it unless the Standard consented to compensation elsewhere. In general, it would be a new departure for Soviet enterprise to cooperate with a capitalist undertaking in a foreign country although the "mixed company" type of concession in Russia where the government shares the work and responsibility of a plant with the foreigner does provide somewhat of a precedent for such an arrangement. If the Standard suggests a similar plan for the United Kingdom—it once did and may again propose a merger with the Russian Oil Products, Ltd., which is a British registered company sponsored by the Naphtha Syndicate—the chances of acceptance would be much better than they are for a partnership in Turkey where Bolshevik prestige might, in the opinion of some, be liable to suffer in the event of a combination with the Americans.

This Turkish situation complicates the discussions with the Socony. But a decision in Moscow to "go the limit" with the Standard would open the door to large sales of Russian oil to the Socony as well as the Soconej, and may even bring Mr. Teagle and his colleagues to Moscow to sue for the Emba concessions.

An attractive feature of the proposed Vacuum purchase was the method of payment. More than anything else the Bolsheviks need money, and the Vacuum Oil Company is prepared to be of considerable assistance to them in this respect. It offered to arrange that large sums be paid in advance to the Syndicate by the Equitable Trust Company of New York City and by other large American banks. The Vacuum suggested that if its purchase would amount to say $5,000,000 during a given period, $1,000,000 or $2,000,000 would be paid by the Equitable to Moscow at the very beginning of that period. The Standard, I understand, is not averse to making similar advances on even more favourable terms should there be a contract not only with the Vacuum but also with the Socony and the Soconej.

This was the position in January, 1926. It was evident that the Standard was quite anxious to come to terms with the Russians, and despite Mr. Teagle's lingering but weakened fear, the Anglo-American representative returned to Europe armed with the authorisation to speak and buy on behalf of the Vacuum, the Socony and the Soconej. The Standard Oil, which had stood like a rock against business dealings with the Soviets, and wrecked the Genoa and Hague conferences, had seen the light.

Conversations between Standard agents and G. Lomov, the president of the Soviet Naphtha Syndicate opened in Berlin in February and continued in

Paris in March. As had been expected, the contract with the Vacuum presented fewest problems and was therefore dispatched first. In the early days of March, an agreement was signed by Lomov and by Charles A. Moser, director of the Vacuum Oil Company, which provided for the sale to the Vacuum of 800,000 tons of Russian crude oil and approximately 100,000 tons of kerosene. Although the terms of this agreement are still secret, it is known that the Vacuum struck an excellent bargain as far as price is concerned and that the Syndicate will not compete with the Vacuum in Egypt where most of the oil contracted for will be marketed.

This is the first commercial transaction between the Soviet Government and an American Standard Oil Company. After eight years of complete abstinence punctuated with active hostility, the Rockefellers, Pratts, Bedfords, etc., have definitely committed themselves to trade with the Bolsheviks. The Vacuum contract, comprehensive and important in itself, is merely the introduction to far more ambitious purchases by the Standard. The negotiators in Paris have now come to grips with the knotty Turkish problem, but the settlement with the Vacuum has established a friendly atmosphere conducive to further business, and there are indications that before long a 100,000-ton purchase by the Socony will be announced which should pave the way to a larger agreement between the Syndicate and the Socony, and ultimately between the Syndicate and the Soconej.

The Socony has made its decision and is exerting

every effort to win Lomov over to the condominium idea in Turkey, for it is clear to the Standard people that they cannot succeed in Angora against Russian opposition and that they would lose a nice penny if they were forced to interrupt the sale of Soviet oil in Turkey and bring liquid over great distances from Mexico or Texas. But before the largest Standard company, the Soconej, takes the momentous plunge, its president, Walter C. Teagle, will look over the ground himself. Teagle announced his departure for Paris in March. He will participate in the pourparlers with the Bolshevik oil men, and Paris may be for him the first stage to Moscow.

The chief justification for Paris as the seat of these negotiations is the desire on the part of all parties to avoid Royal Dutch-Shell obstruction in London. Sir Henri Deterding is anxious to see the Standard-Soviet conversations break down, in order that his Royal Dutch remain the only large prospect for the Moscow Syndicate, in which case he could, he believes, dictate his own terms. For this reason he has been untiring in his efforts to torpedo the Paris meetings. The Vacuum and the Socony can afford to take little notice of him. He can do them slight harm. But Deterding can threaten Teagle with a "price war" which would reverberate throughout the whole oil world.

This possibility may deter the Soconej, but the latest indications from Paris are that it will not. The die seems to be cast, and, if straws show which way the wind blows, the entire Standard organisation will soon be on the ledgers of the Soviet Naphtha Syndicate.

It is not precluded that the Royal Dutch-Shell will also enter the transaction. There is precedent for Standard purchases from the Russians on which the Shell may exercise an option, and the same arrangement, plus a few stray concessions from the Standard elsewhere, may appease the wily Deterding and persuade him to bury the hatchet. He bought oil from the Syndicate and very likely will again. To him it is a question of pounds, shillings and pence. And if Teagle offers him and his associates sufficient inducement, they will be reconciled. Meanwhile evidence has come to hand which proves beyond dispute that the Rockefeller trust has definitely unfurled the pro-Russian flag. *The Standard Oil is advocating recognition of Soviet Russia by the United States.*

On March 27, 1926, *The New York Times* published the following cable from Paris:

"The Standard Oil Company of New York and the Vacuum Oil Company have just completed negotiations with the Soviet Government of Russia for the purchases of 190,000 tons of refined oil at $17 a ton, or a total of more than $3,200,000."

On the following day, under the caption "Ivy Lee Moved to Aid the Soviet," the front page of the *Times* blurted out the following announcement:

"Ivy L. Lee, the best-known and most expensive of publicity agents, who, among other activities, is the 'adviser on public relations' of the Standard Oil Company, has begun to display keen interest in the recognition of the Soviet Government of Russia by the United States. Mr. Lee, it was learned yesterday, is so greatly interested that he has sent out a series of 'confidential letters' to prominent men in relation to the matter, among them to the former Secretary of State Elihu Root."

On March 3, 1926, Mr. Lee wrote to Mr. Root:

"It would seem that the policy of drift with reference to Russia was getting us nowhere, and that the problem after all was a very practical one which had to be settled after consideration of all the practical questions involved, with a view to bringing about as permanent results the promotion of the peace, security and financial stability of the world. . . . I would never want this country to recognise Russia if you yourself—after examining all the facts—should deem it unwise. *What I would like to see, however, is a condition brought about under which you, and men like you, would think it wise to accord such recognition.*"

An executive of the New York State Chamber of Commerce received the following suggestion from the same source:

"Some day Russia has got to come back into the family of nations, and we ought to try to help her get back rather than to force a great nation like Russia to come back on her knees and in sackcloth and ashes. That isn't practical. Furthermore, the United States cannot indefinitely assume an attitude toward Russia different from that of all the other great nations. In addition, the trade of Russia is of great importance to this country."

Throughout this correspondence, which has assumed

voluminous proportions, the recognition of Russia by Britain, France and Italy, and the consequent isolation of the United States, is repeatedly emphasised by Mr. Lee.

"Many business concerns have been conducting negotiations with a view to the reestablishment of more active commercial relations in Russia. One very large American interest last summer was, as a basis for the establishment of trade relations in Russia, consulting with the foreign secretaries of England and France with a view to ascertaining the probable policy of those countries as to their continued recognition of Russia. . . . I am informed quite definitely that it is not the purpose of any of the great nations of Europe to withdraw such recognition."

The same subject recurs in a letter under date of February 15, 1926, to the president of a powerful financial institution:

"It seems to me that when a nation has been recognised by governments like England and France, it is rather difficult for the United States to maintain that the moral principles which surround us are different from those which govern the governments of England and France, and that we have a right to take a more elevated position in the matter than these other nations. To be sure, Russia was recognised by England while under the control of a Labour government, but it is equally certain that the Tory government has resisted all efforts to withdraw the recognition of Russia which had been given by the Labour government. My personal opinion is that there is not the slightest prospect of the recognition of Russia being withdrawn by either England, France or Italy."

No one could suspect this spokesman of the Rockefeller interests of sympathy with Communism. Nevertheless, he is at pains to make his position clear:

"No one has less sympathy than I have with any government or organisation which advocates Communism or seeks to stimulate a world revolution. . . .

"The real problem, as I see it, is not whether the present party in control of the Russian government represents views which we can endorse, or whether the Russian government ought not to be severely condemned. Theoretically and logically, we ought to do everything possible to keep the Russian government 'thumbs down'. But it is not a theory which confronts us; it is a very real fact. From our point of view, we want to trade with Russia. We not only want to trade ourselves, but we want other nations to trade with them and thus promote world prosperity. We have got to recognise that so far as Russia is concerned, it represents an enormous population whose restoration to an orderly society is of supreme importance to the progress of civilisation.

"As I view it, therefore, the real question is this: How can Russia be once more restored to the family of nations, so that her full contribution may be made to the welfare of the world?"

Such a campaign naturally met with some opposition. This was to be expected, since it was directed primarily to persons who were most hostile to the Soviet government. Mr. Elihu Root replies to express his fear of the "demoralisation of public opinion throughout the United States", should his country extend the hand of courtesy to the Russian people. The head of a company which suffered losses through the Revolution makes fervent objection. Each one receives a soft answer to turn away wrath: "I am not the least afraid of the Russian government having agencies in this country who will circulate subversive propaganda. . . . If the Russian government had diplomatic agents in this country, everything they did would be subjected to the most careful supervision and the public would be on guard against them constantly. Such agents, knowing that they were under suspicion, would be extremely careful as to what they did." As for the "moral aspects" of the question: "I am afraid, if it is to be dealt with purely on a plane of higher morality, we are not going to get very far." Russia should make restitution for property seized from foreigners and give guarantees of normal commercial relations in the future. "That is a very practical question and cannot be solved merely by our disapproving of the professions and theories of the Russian government."

To the super-patriots who urge support of the State Department's policy, Mr. Lee retorts: "The State Department may be wrong! But right or wrong, I do not believe that the policy of the State Department should be endorsed *merely* because *it is* the policy of the State Department. Nor do I think that we should assume that the State Department has inside information which justifies its policy. It may or may not have." Again he says: "It seems to me there is nothing in experience to justify the claim that the policy so far followed by our State Department will get us anywhere."

The origin and purpose of this letter-writing campaign, coincident with the negotiations in Paris, is well known in Wall Street and in Washington. It has even been brought discreetly to the attention of Moscow as though the accomplished scribe did not wish his friendly efforts to pass unnoticed in that quarter, where the knowledge of such activities might promote the interests of his clients. Throughout the correspondence there is not the slightest mention of oil. But the odour of petroleum clings heavily about the stationery on which it is written.

The Standard has a far reach. The left hand works for political recognition in the United States, while the right hand bargains for millions of tons of oil in Paris.[9]

[9] On March 26, 1926, the Paris correspondent of *The New York Times* cabled:

"The French company with which the Standard Oil is affiliated explained today that the American purchase of Russian oil is very advantageous. Oil will be sold in Egypt and Turkey and the cost of transport will be much less than if the oil were brought from an American port.

"The same officials, while not admitting that the purchase indicated a change in Russian policy on the part of American industry, explained that if Russia offered more oil and it seemed good business, American firms probably would not hesitate to buy."

On the same day the London correspondent of *The Wall Street Journal* cabled:

"The arrival of Walter C. Teagle, president of Standard Oil Company of New Jersey, is looked forward to with great interest in European oil circles as a visit likely to lead to a settlement of a number of troublesome oil conflicts. . . . There is the question of purchasing Russian oil. Vacuum, closely connected with Standard, bought nearly 100,000 tons recently. New York Standard is negotiating. However, Mr. Teagle is more reluctant to deal in any kind of oil about which there might be questions raised as to ownership. . . . With such big issues at stake Mr. Teagle very understandably did not make the usual bromide answer as to the purpose of his trip abroad by saying 'off on a holiday'."

CHAPTER VI

SOVIET CONCESSIONS

It is one of the saddest phenomena of the bourgeois world that the interests which ought to link together to form a united front against their mortal enemies, the Bolsheviks, are always torn apart by inner dissensions. In the fullness of their hatred for one another, the capitalists have never been able to drown their differences and combine in a common hatred against the expropriating Soviets. It was so easy to play one trust against the other that the blockade which was to have brought Russia to her knees before them ended in complete failure.

We have seen how one-half of the blockade-line crumbled because Russian oil is indispensable to the European market. The desire of the petroleum companies for Soviet concessions completely destroyed the other half, leaving nothing but inchoate débris as a monument to the "disloyalty" of oil magnates to their confrères and their own pledges.

The Groupement was but an infant, it will be recalled, when its very members sabotaged all efforts to maintain a common anti-Soviet policy. They did so, not merely by placing orders for Caucasian kerosene with Moscow agents, but also by sending emissaries into the enemy camp to make overtures for contracts and leases. The Royal Dutch-Shell was the most aggressive group in this respect. There was many an occasion when its negotiations with Russian envoys in London and elsewhere seemed to have advanced so far that the press hastened to announce the actual signing of a concession. In each case, however, the news item was premature. All Deterding's efforts ended in failures.

The Royal Dutch invariably assured itself the support of the British government. This was patent enough at Genoa. If it was not, we have Sir Austen Chamberlain's own words uttered in the House of Commons on May 9, 1922, when he replied in the affirmative to an M. P.'s question as to whether the negotiations which "have recently taken place between the oil combination known as the Royal Dutch-Shell and the Soviet government of Russia . . . were with the sanction of His Majesty's government." But despite the friendly aid of Downing Street nothing positive was achieved.

The Royal Dutch was not the only bidder. In 1922 we find the Anglo-Maikop Corporation, a combine of eight oil companies, applying for a concession and listening to a report that "the board consider themselves entitled to take a favourable view as to the outcome." [1] But there was no favourable outcome. Again, "The two private French oil missions which had gone to Moscow and then to Baku in order to obtain oil

[1] *Oil News,* July 8, 1922.

concessions have returned to France. It is announced that they have been unable to reach a satisfactory agreement with the government of the Soviets." [2] These are but a few of the many who tried and did not succeed. The Bolsheviks, apparently, were not easily persuaded to part with their petroleum wealth.

The attempt of the Standard Oil deserves special attention. In the winter of 1923, we have noted, Mr. Dodge, an important official of the Standard, appeared in Moscow and remained there for several weeks. The last Royal Dutch-Soviet negotiation had ended, with nothing, in November of the previous year. The Standard Oil, therefore, considered the time opportune and the circumstances favourable for a bid of its own. The fact that Mr. Dodge and his Scandinavian companion and interpreter were permitted to enter Russia is sufficient proof that the Soviets were prepared to listen to a Standard offer. But the Rockefeller company's bid was based on a claim to Baku. The attitude of Messrs. Teagle and Bedford had always been that the oil properties which they had bought from Nobel were their possession. Mr. Dodge came to ascertain whether the Bolsheviks were ripe to restitute these fields. *He* would, if compelled, make certain concessions to the government. It was not, however, a matter of applying for a concession from the Soviet government. What Dodge, in effect, asked for was the denationalisation of the Baku fields which his company had "acquired" by its transaction from Nobel. Nothing more.

[2] *Daily Telegraph*, June 26, 1923.

Now there was only one small difficulty. The Soviets did not recognise the Standard's claim to any property in Baku. The position of the Moscow government on this matter is, and was, very clear. Nobel was a Russian citizen. When the Russian state nationalised his property in the Caucasus, it ceased to belong to him, and he was accordingly in no position to sell it. That he did sell it is no concern of the Bolsheviks. His customer was the loser.

The attitude of the Russians on this subject has never altered. To be sure, they were ready to entertain a Standard Oil application for a concession, just as they entertained tenders from Harriman, Sinclair, and other organisations which had never had any interests in Russia before the revolution. But any private deal which the Standard Oil and Nobel had entered into somewhere in London, Paris, or New York would not receive consideration. If the Rockefeller family was deprived of a few millions by this heartless Bolshevik judgment, that was its punishment for not taking the nationalisation act seriously and for speculating on the overthrow of the Soviets by a power which would be more considerate of the claims of capitalists.

Needless to say, Mr. Dodge and his superiors did not share these views. The Standard Oil still has a map of the Baku oil-field on which its own possessions are marked in red, or perhaps black. The Soviet government, of course, cannot stop the Standard Oil directors from believing that they continue to hold property in the Caucasus, but it never had any intention of altering its plans simply because the Standard Oil, and other companies, insist on nursing worthless papers.

It is hard to believe that the Standard Oil people still expect the Bolsheviks to denationalise their property in Russia. Yet till recently former Secretary of State Hughes insisted on denationalisation as a condition of United States recognition of the Soviet republic. Mr. Hughes was always ready to use his position to fight the battles of the Standard Oil. He did so, on the Mesopotamian question, at Genoa and The Hague, and in Persia under the convenient cover of the "open door" policy. There is much justice, therefore, in the suspicion of Russian authorities that Hughes' stubborn refusal to recognise the Soviets was directly associated with the fate of the Standard Oil's holdings in Baku, and that all his indignant moralistic philippics against Moscow were really a smoke screen for the State Department's desire to obtain satisfaction through denationalisation for the Rockefeller interests.

This was, no doubt, an important factor in the attitude of Hughes to Russia. But that it should today influence America's Russian policy is altogether inconceivable. In the first place, a restitution of the Standard Oil's claimed property in the Caucasus is about as imminent as a Communist dictatorship in the United States. Moreover, there are signs that in 1925 the Standard Oil itself commenced to question the probability of the return of its property by the Russian State. Its offer to purchase the entire product of

Baku over a period of.years was one such indication.

The Washington government may now find it difficult to overcome the inertia of eight years of non-recognition. Then, too, affairs in the Far East, in China particularly, may yet suggest to the State Department that caution is the better part of wisdom, but it is to be hoped that regard for the Standard Oil no longer plays a rôle in the situation. It has done so, too long already. A few more months will perhaps disillusion the Rockefeller directors entirely, and move them to write off their transaction with Nobel as a complete, dead loss.

A few years ago, however, the Standard Oil must never have thought for a moment of such an eventuality. Great, therefore, was its chagrin when it heard that its most serious domestic rival, Harry F. Sinclair, had actually applied for a concession to all the petroleum resources of the Caucasus.

Mr. Sinclair should not be underestimated. He had vision and an eye to the future. His company was light and adaptable because of its speculative character. Moreover, the man whose name it carries has ambition. And he was not wrong in looking towards Russia. For Russia offered him the possibility of becoming the greatest oil monarch in the world, a station more to be desired than the throne of Albania.

His chances of getting a concession were undoubtedly good. Sinclair had not been a partner to the blockade decision. He had never had any interests in Russia and, therefore, had no claims. He was far less considerate than most oil magnates of the claims of former foreign owners. He had no entangling alliances which might have introduced political factors objectionable to the Communists. Moreover, the Soviets at that time were in a very receptive mood. They were anxious to lease Baku and Grosni. Finally, Sinclair was an American; there was, therefore, a possibility of loans and credits, and possibly even of recognition of Moscow by the American government.

The Soviets understand right well that the oil of the Caucasus is a valuable and much desired asset. When they were inclined to lease it to foreigners they wished to gain not only economical but political advantages as well by doing so. And just as they had made the Sakhalien concession to Sinclair [3] contingent upon United States recognition, so they expected at least as much for the more extensive, richer, and better developed petroleum fields of the Caucasus.

Sinclair was not without his friends in the executive mansions of the American government. The minutes of the Senate investigation of the Teapot Dome scandal testify amply to this fact. Messrs. Daugherty and Denby, now besmirched by their deeds, were then still members of the United States cabinet. Warren G. Harding was president. He was a close acquaintance of Harry F. It would be a disparagement to Mr. Sinclair to suppose that he, the clever bargainer, did not use these connections as one of his big cards in the negotiations with the Soviet representatives. Indeed, he would have been in his right to assure Maxim Litvinov, who conducted the negotiations on behalf of the

[3] See chapter vii, "The United States, Japan and Russia".

Bolsheviks, that he had considerable influence in Washington and that he would use it to bring about a reestablishment of normal diplomatic relations between the two countries.

This was not merely as a favour for a favour received. Recognition was an absolutely necessary preliminary to the Sinclair concession. In the first place the Sakhalien concession depended on it. In the second place he needed American diplomatic protection in Russia. The Bolsheviks were asking Sinclair for a $250,000,000 loan. Furthermore, Sinclair would have had to invest scores of millions in the gigantic concessions which were contemplated. Now no business man risks hundreds of millions of dollars in a land where his government has no ambassador and where, therefore, he can expect only as much redress of grievances as the interested state is willing to grant. From every angle from which the Sinclair bid is viewed, it becomes clear that it entailed United States recognition.[4] The Bolsheviks wanted it and Sinclair had to have it.

The Sinclair party, which arrived in London in June, 1923, consisted of Harry F. Sinclair, Senator Fall, Mason Day, Archibald B. Roosevelt, Robert Law, Jr., Wm. Dewey Loucks, E. R. Tinker, Elisha Walker, Grattan T. Stanford, and two mining engineers. Sinclair stated to Krassin that his wish was to take over the entire oil industry of Russia—Baku, Grosni,

[4] Litvinov, always the diplomat, tells me that he did not discuss American recognition with Sinclair, but that he assumed that Sinclair would not enter upon so large an undertaking in Russia without the approval of the United States government. Such approval, had it been forthcoming, would in the opinion of Litvinov, ultimately have led to recognition.

Emba, Maikop, and every other field. But that was not all. He desired to have a refining monopoly. He wanted to build pipe-lines, to erect plants. He offered to sell oil in Russia and to be the sole distributor abroad of Russian oil products.

Krassin had to bring Sinclair back to earth. The Soviets were prepared to give Sinclair a concession but not one so ambitious and inclusive. It was too great a power, economic and therefore political, to place in the hands of a single company. Accordingly, Krassin proposed, as an alternative to the wholesale concession idea, a more limited agreement which would include a contract for Emba, the laying of some pipe-lines, the sale of oil abroad, the construction of a paraffin-separating plant and an arrangement for boring some wells at Baku and Grosni.

Now at this time the French were now in Moscow discussing a concession for Emba with the Chief Concessions Committee. Furthermore, the Bolsheviks had early that year ruled that binding negotiations looking to oil concessions could be conducted only in Moscow. It therefore became necessary for the Sinclair party to proceed to the Red capital. This it did. Harry F. and the court which trailed behind him was cordially received in Moscow, housed in a palace, dined, supplied with special railway cars, etc.

After a sojourn of a month or so, the leader of the expedition left Russia with several members of the party, not, however, before the general outline and many of the details of an important concession had been agreed upon between Sinclair and the Soviet leaders.

Mr. Mason Day, Sinclair's European representative, remained in Moscow to conclude the agreement.

In a comparatively short time—as time is reckoned in Soviet concession negotiations—a provisional agreement was signed in Moscow by Mason Day, and by Litvinov for the Soviet government. This was in the early part of November, 1923. The concession provided for the organisation of a mixed company in which the Soviet government and the Sinclair Corporation held equal shares. The Soviet government invested the fields and their equipment, while Sinclair invested 230,-000,000 gold roubles (approximately $115,000,000). The concession covered the oil-fields of Grosni and Baku, and provided for the sale of oil products by the mixed company on both the domestic and foreign markets. The management would be equally divided and so also the profits. Sinclair would receive interest on his capital, and the government amortisation on its property. The duration of the concession was forty-nine years.

The agreement stipulated, moreover, that Sinclair was to float a loan for Russia or for some Russian industrial enterprise in New York. The document signed by Mason Day stated that the agreement was to be confirmed by Sinclair within forty-five days, and that forty-five additional days were allowed before the final signature of the concession contract.

Now Sinclair and the Standard Oil were sharp competitors in the United States. Sinclair had also given the Standard much trouble in Persia. As a matter of fact, he had actually taken a concession in that country to an oil-field on which the Standard still held an option.[5] And here he was in Russia again poaching on Rockefeller's preserves. For obviously, if Sinclair accepted a lease to all of Baku, the part of Baku which the Standard Oil claimed would have come under his control. It would have been foolhardy to expect the Standard Oil to sit by idly and permit this "upstart in the petroleum industry" to outmanœuvre it on every turn.

Sinclair felt that this was the logic of the situation. He told one of his representatives in Moscow that he feared a "Nemesis would pursue him" on account of his activities in Russia. When the Sinclair company entered a bid for a field which the Standard Oil considered its own, it was indeed on dangerous ground; it was like stepping in where angels feared to tread. And woe to the man who offends the mighty Standard.

Only a few months after Sinclair's Russian trip, the Teapot Dome scandal came to light. Senator Walsh's committee, which undertook to investigate it, unearthed facts that not only disgraced United States officialdom in the eyes of the world, revealing its venality and corruption, it not merely disclosed the unscrupulousness of oil companies, but was the direct cause of the removal from the president's cabinet of Secretaries Denby and Daugherty, Sinclair's best "pals." Moreover, the investigation seriously damaged his credit on the open market. He could no more float a $250,000,-000 loan than he could compete for the grand prix for honesty.

[5] See chapter viii, "In the Shahdom of Persia".

These developments were the end of a series of disasters the first of which was the unexpected demise of President Harding. With Harding dead, and Denby and Daugherty disgraced, Sinclair was as little able to deliver United States recognition to Russia as he was of getting the Bolsheviks a quarter billion dollars in Wall Street. The affair of the Teapot Dome in Wyoming also closed the Sinclair chapter on the Caucasus, for after it Sinclair was in no position to honour either his own promises in Moscow or the signature which his agent, Mason Day, had attached to the agreement made in the Soviet capital.

The Standard Oil was undoubtedly pleased, and the busy directors must have heaved a sigh of relief. If they themselves had staged the scandal, or if they themselves had obliquely suggested the investigation to some friend of a secretary of a senator—and there are suspicions that this was the case—the results achieved could not have been more favourable for them. Before the scandal there was the possibility that Sinclair would grow to giant proportions through his acquisitions in Soviet Russia. After it his chances in Baku were reduced to nil.. His stocks in Persia also fell. In fine, the chief domestic rival of the Standard had shrunk to dwarf stature and was ready for the rôle of those many "independents" who are in truth mere satellitic subsidiaries of the great mogul of the American and world oil industry.

Since the passing of Sinclair no candidate for important oil concessions in the Caucasus has appeared on the Soviet horizon. Meanwhile, increased productivity, greater efficiency—which still, however, leaves much room for improvement—and growing profits, mark the government operations in Baku and Grosni. Grosni has already exceeded its pre-war output, and Baku is fast approaching the ante-bellum norm. These developments, coupled as they have been with a favourable domestic and foreign market, have given the Bolsheviks heart. Russian leaders now declare that Baku and Grosni are working so well that no thought of leasing them to foreigners is being entertained. These fields—the richest in Russia—shall continue under state control and management. This describes the general feeling I met with in Baku in October, 1924, and in Moscow before that and after.

To be sure, this decision is neither final nor irrevocable. As A. E. Minckin, the secretary of the Chief Concessions Committee, once said to the writer, "Everything depends on the political and economic advantages which are offered us in consideration of a concession." In other words, every oil-field has its price. But as the months and years go by, the price of Baku and Grosni rise, and they will be unattainable very soon if they are not already so now.

Shortly after the Russo-Japanese treaty was signed in January, 1925, rumours commenced to circulate regarding the possible leasing of Baku to a semi-government Japanese petroleum concern. However, though the rumours persisted for several months, it appears that they had no basis in fact. A prediction on the general subject would be foolhardy, for events may any day dictate a modification of policy, but there is much reason to suppose that the Moscow government will not permit Baku and Grosni to pass out of its hands.

With respect to Emba the official attitude is different. Emba is a large and potentially rich field whose resources have hardly been tapped. To develop it and to equip it with modern machinery and plants would require considerable capital. Moreover, the field lies in a desert and is practically devoid of railroad connections and pipe-line facilities. Finally, water must be brought to it. There can be no doubt that a few years' operation would amply repay any investment made in Emba, but the Soviet government has no available funds for the purpose and is hardly likely to come into possession of them in the near future. For this reason Emba is on the market. At one time there were reports that the Shell Company was anxious to acquire the field. For some years a French corporation has been most active in courting the Bolsheviks for the concession. Representatives of the company have spent months in the Hotel Savoy in Moscow negotiating and bargaining with Soviet officials. The concern controls much French industrial and commercial capital, and its efforts are said to enjoy the support of the Paris government. Nevertheless, the concession has as yet not been granted.

Until the spring of 1925 the Bolsheviks pursued a hyper-cautious concessions policy. The appointment of Leon Trotsky, as chairman of the Chief Concessions Committee, signalised a decided change in the government's attitude and tactics. He had no sooner assumed office than the two largest concessions ever granted by Communist Russia were signed in Moscow, the one with the Anglo-American Lena Goldfields Company, the other with W. A. Harriman, of New York, for the invaluable manganese deposits of Chiaturi, in the republic of Georgia. These two contracts, Trotsky himself stated, "signify the opening of a period of accelerated concessions activity. We, fully conscious, are meeting it halfway." [6] Concessions, he declared, on the same occasion, "have until recently played an all too minor rôle in our economic life. The capitalists, misled by their own press, hoped that under the pressure of necessity we would offer them better and better terms. They argued thus: Tomorrow a concession will cost us less than it does today, and the day after tomorrow it can perhaps be obtained for nothing. This explains the comparatively weak development of our concessions activity. We, ourselves, were very cautious, too cautious we may say, in our concessions negotiations." How much this modification of policy will affect the granting of oil concessions still remains to be seen. In the meantime, aside from the Japanese concession on Northern Sakhalien, only two oil leases have been signed between the Soviet government and foreign capital. Neither of these are important but they must form part of the record. The first is a contract to an Italo-Belgian firm with a capital of 1,500,000 gold lire. It gives the company the right to explore for oil in the southern Siberian steppes. The second is to the

[6] Statement made by Trotsky to a German workingmen's delegation, July, 1925.

Norwegian Corporation of F. Stoeren. The concession is for a period of forty years and grants permission to explore for and drill oil in the peninsula of Busachi, which extends from the northeastern coast of the Caspian. This concession has a promising future. The district covered is geologically a part of the Baku field and is said to be rich in fine oil. In January, 1926, it was reported from Oslo that the company had explored 12,000 square kilometres near Kaidak Bay, in the east Caspian, and discovered oil. Boring operations were scheduled to commence in the summer of 1926.

It is this type of minor concession which the Bolsheviks are ready and even anxious to grant to foreign capital. On the periphery of that vast expanse which is the Soviet Union there are numerous territories abounding in petroleum which have either been exploited at one time and subsequently abandoned, or partially explored and known to contain the liquid. In his *Petroleum Resources of the World*, Valentine R. Garfias, petroleum engineer of the United States Bureau of Mines, mentions oil deposits at Naphtha Gora, 100 miles inland from Krasnovodsk on the Caspian where there has been some production since 1881, Ferghana in Central Asia which until 1926 was an important though second-rate producer of Russian oil, Archangel in North Russia, Daghestan, the province of Kutais in the Republic of Georgia, Saratov and Samara governments, the Turgai in Western Siberia, the region around Lake Baikal and the Amur River in Eastern Siberia, Kertch in the Crimea, and Anapa near the shores of the Sea of Azov. But this does not exhaust the list. Oil indications have also been discovered at Melitopol in the Ukraine, near Gudermos in the vicinity of Rostov-on-the-Don, and in the Peninsula of Kamchatka for the resources of which, it will be remembered, the American, Washington D. Vanderlip, tried, in 1920, to obtain a concession. Mention must likewise be made of Holy (Sviatoi) Island in the Caspian, of Cheleken Island in the same sea which, during 1921, yielded 200,000 tons of petroleum, and of the Sapsa-Notanev area between Batum and Poti on the Black Sea coast.[7]

The Soviet government is particularly anxious to bring some of these fields under exploitation. A circular letter dated August 21, 1925, from the Concessions Committee of the Moscow Supreme Economic Council to its foreign representatives, states the reason with characteristic Bolshevik frankness. The letter calls attention to the increasing demand abroad for Soviet oil and to the pressing problem of enlarging Russia's petroleum yield in order to take full advantage of this favourable world market conjuncture. But "the necessity of expending large sums on preliminary explorations and drilling without sufficient guarantee of success does not permit our state institutions to enter upon such work on a sufficiently large scale. For this reason the attraction of foreign capital for the exploration of new areas is considered altogether desir-

---

[7] This area the Soviet Government intends reserving for its own purposes in connection with the refineries soon to be constructed at Batum.

able. In order to stimulate the activity of foreign companies they must—in the event of a successful issue of their explorations—be accorded the right to exploit a certain fraction of the investigated territory. . . ."

The fields which are suggested as objects for concessions or as the scenes of preliminary exploration which is to be followed by a contract for exploitation are:

1. *Cheleken Island.* In 1911 there were sixty-six producing wells; in 1917, thirty-seven. The equipment of the field is now almost completely worthless.

2. *Naphtha Gora* (Neftedag) in the Trans-Caspian. "The region," says the circular, "is clearly petroliferous but it is situated among sands and remote from inhabited parts. Considerable expense would be required for exploration and initial equipment. In the '80's of the last century five wells were sunk here. Several of these yielded 600 poods a day at a depth of 50-60 sazhen."

3. *The Derbent area* (Daghestan), stretching from the city of Derbent on the west coast of the Caspian north for a distance of forty kilometres. There are eight known fields of which Kaya-Kent, where three groups of wells have been worked, and Berekee, where thirty wells have been drilled, are the most promising. Gusher oil has been obtained in both places. To date, 4,000,000 poods have been produced at Berekee.

4. *The Kertch Peninsula.* The region is explored and some oil has been produced.

5. *Kakhetia* in Georgia—the home of the world-famous wine. The petroliferous area extends for 200

kilometres parallel to the Tiflis-Elizavetopol railway. Investigators have found oil in several places, but the explorations were never completed.

6. The *Uchta* district in Archangel in the valley of the Uchta River. Wells sunk at four different places have yielded petroleum.

7. *Izbekstan* in Central Asia. This is the *Ferghana* field for the Sel Rokh and Tchiminion areas of which have been worked with a profit in the past.

In most of the areas enumerated in the circular letter, operations on a commercial scale seem to have a fair chance of success but in all, except Cheleken and Ferghana, perhaps, further explorations will have to be conducted. All, moreover, require considerable capital investment. But the circular correctly emphasises the fact that the regions it suggests as objects of concessions are without exception very favourably placed with respect to export. This is particularly true of Cheleken, Derbent, Kertch, Kakhetia and Uchta. Cheleken has the additional advantage of being so situated as to enable the prospective concessionaire to make use of the refining and transport facilities of Baku, while Derbent can avail itself of the factories and pipe-lines of either Grosni or Baku.

During the past several years, the Soviet government has entertained numerous bids from companies desiring oil concessions in Russia. On one occasion in 1925 when I asked Minckin, the secretary of the Chief Concessions Committee, whether they were examining any offers for oil-fields from foreign groups, he replied, "Yes, about sixty, just at present." The number fluctuates but it is never small. Some are not serious. I am reminded of one naïve soul, an Englishman, who thought that because he had sat in Brixton prison with Chicherin during the war the Moscow authorities ought surely give him a petroleum concession. Some are unacceptable. This was the nature of an offer made by the Baku Consolidated Company of London, through its intermediary, Mr. Rickett, which was a poorly-veiled request for restitution of its properties in Baku. Similarly, the Gadjinsky Cheleken Company of London applied in January, 1923, for properties on Cheleken "of which we are the owners." But since the Soviets do not recognise any ownership to nationalised property except their own, such an application could hardly form the basis for discussion.

It would be a tiresome and uninteresting task to enumerate the many English, French, Belgian, Swedish, Italian and American corporations which have, at one time or another, courted the Petrol Section of Moscow's Chief Concessions Committee or of its agents abroad. Suffice it to say that none but two, and the Japanese in Sakhalien, have succeeded.[8] The Soviets set severe and sometimes impossible conditions, and it is, no doubt, a most difficult matter finally to close a deal with them. The Bolsheviks are astute negotiators and endlessly patient bargainers, so much so that they often drive the foreigner to desperation and his own home.

[8] The arrangement with the American Barnsdall Corporation, which was permitted to lapse by mutual consent in 1924, was not properly an oil concession as the company was really nothing more than a contractor who drilled wells for the Baku trust.

Moscow may prove more reasonable in the matter of minor concessions adumbrated in the circular letter quoted above. But with respect to the five first-class Russian oil-fields, the would-be concessionaire has a long and thorny path to tread.

The oil-fields referred to are (1) Baku, (2) Grosni, (3) Emba, (4) Maikop, and (5) Sakhalien.

(1) Baku is a profitable and going business. There is little reason why the Soviets should lease it to a foreigner. To be sure, Baku needs money. Refineries require new installations. A new pipe-line to Batum should supplement the one carrying only kerosene which is in use today. Acreage outside the borders of the areas now under exploitation ought to be explored and opened up. But the Azerbaijhan Naphtha Trust (Azneft) which operates this largest of Russian fields has registered considerable progress in recent years. Machinery to the value of millions of dollars is annually being imported from the United States. The greater part of Baku has been electrified with equipment brought from America. The construction of a model refinery in Batum is contemplated. The Bibi Ebat field, one of Baku's most promising districts, is being pushed out into the sea while the water is filled in, and some of the most powerful of the Azneft's gushers have sprung from where, only a few months before, the breakers of the salty Caspian ruled supreme. If it were not in Soviet Russia, the Azneft, as a profit-earning organisation with an excellent market and a bright future, would experience no trouble in obtaining credits and loans on the bourses of the world. With

many oil companies and a few governments still hostile, however, it must struggle along and move forward at a slackened pace making improvements out of that part of its earnings which the central government does not attach.

Nevertheless, a Baku concession becomes an increasing improbability as each month the economic strength of the Azneft grows. Moreover, State operation has definitely proved the advantage of single, unified management over the chaotic, competitive system of management by many companies owning large and small parcels of land, with the result that only a few giant trusts are eligible for such a tremendous undertaking as the exploitation of the entire Baku field. British corporations are further handicapped by political considerations, for there is among the Bolsheviks an extremely influential body of opinion which would oppose most strenuously any concession giving an English concern a foothold in so strategically important a region as the Caucasus. My own view is that Baku will never go to a foreign capitalist except in the event of a long, extremely threatening and at present unlikely economic crisis in all of Soviet Russia.

(2) The same applies to Grosni. In fact, this can be asserted of Grosni, with even greater certainty, for the Grosni field has exceeded pre-war production and is passing through a period of rapid expansion. [9] The

[9] On the professed assumption that the Soviet government would, in the near future, restitute its properties in Grosni and compensate it for the losses to the company in consequence of the revolution, the Spies Petroleum Company, on January 18, 1926, held a special meeting to rearrange its capital in order to obtain more funds from old and prospective shareholders. This

Grosni-Tuapse pipe-line will add to its earning capacity and value.

(3) The Soviets can allocate only very limited means at present for the development of Emba. At best they can maintain production at the level at which it now stands. According to one report, the intention is to drill only five new boreholes during the 1925-26 fiscal year. This is very far from enough. All agree that Emba has the makings of one of the world's greatest oil-fields, but much more money will have to be poured into it if its potentialities are to be realised. The Soviet government is, therefore, quite anxious to deliver this field into the hands of a wealthy foreign conces-sionaire. Years of pourparlers with the French have been fruitless. The indications are that Moscow would welcome a bid from an American firm, perhaps even from the Standard Oil. . . . (Emba produced 98,289 tons in 1913, 125,500 in 1923-24, and 128,000 tons in 1924-25.)

(4) Maikop has been badly neglected by the Soviet government. Neither Moscow nor many prospective

money, the officers of the Spies announced, was required so that the company would be in a position to accept the property as soon as the Bolsheviks returned it. Yet it must be clear to the directors, as it is patent to any student of the situation, that the Spies Petroleum would be the last likely candidate for a concession to Grosni even if the Russians were prepared to grant one, and there is not the slightest indication that they are. Moreover, the new scheme of the Spies directors to "obtain requisite financial support" for themselves is predicated on the readiness of the Moscow government not only to restitute but to compensate as well. But I think too highly of the intelligence of at least one of the chief officials of Spies to suppose that he and his colleagues for a moment entertain any illusions on the possibility of their property being restituted and their company being compensated by the Bolsheviks.

concessionaires have paid much attention to it. Operations have been left to the local authorities who had neither the money nor the organisation to carry on the work. The result has been that the field yields far less today than it did before the war. Moreover, much of the equipment requires replacement. The central government in Moscow somewhat belatedly—in December, 1925—realised the necessity of taking drastic measures in order to prevent Maikop from seriously depreciating in value, and made the field a ward of the Grosni Oil Trust (Grosneft) which had been instructed to take immediate steps to raise production. There is every reason to believe that the Soviets would not close their hearts to an attractive foreign offer for Maikop but, in the absence of such a one, and in view of the increasing demand for Soviet oil, both at home and abroad, the government will soon have to proceed with intensive exploitation itself.

(5) The Sakhalien concession and its international complications are discussed in the next chapter.

CHAPTER VII

THE UNITED STATES, JAPAN, AND RUSSIA

THE Locarno Pact and the League of Nations' acts notwithstanding, most of the world's epochal history during the last year has been made in the Far East, particularly in China. Even if one were prone to overlook or forget the rôle of Soviet Russia in the Chinese situation, the daily newspapers do not permit it; they are on their guard. There is the "Red Peril", "Karakhan and His Money", "Feng, the 'Christian General' Turned Bolshevik", the "Russo-Japanese-Chinese Bloc", and a score of other scare headlines with which to shock, startle, and stun their readers.

It is impossible to overemphasise the importance of the great drama which is being enacted on the distant coast of the Pacific. And it is equally difficult to exaggerate the part which Moscow is playing in it. Authorities and observers agree that if it were not for the Russian Revolution of 1917 the Chinese revolution may have come as early as 1925. Certainly its forms and expressions would have been different. China is fighting with her back to the wall against the aggression of foreign imperialism. Russia is the outstanding example of a country which, by revolution, succeeded in extricating itself from outside domination. China is tupanised, tuchunised, cut and sliced up among provincial war lords, many of them supported or instigated by world Powers whose interests are not a unified yellow nation. The Russia of 1918 and 1919 was in a similar position. But the Bolsheviks expelled the Koltchaks, Denikins, Petluras, Semenovs, Yudenitches, etc., despite the tanks, money, uniforms, advice, ammunition and generals which Europe and America showered upon them. The Chinese intelligentsia, student movement and Nationalists are anxious to emulate the Communist example even though they may not be prepared as yet to accept the teachings of Marx and Lenin. What could be more natural?

Under these circumstances, and in view of the moral assistance and encouragement which the Russians are happy and anxious to give China in her struggle, the close friendship which has developed between the two countries is not to be marvelled at. It would even be correct, perhaps, to say that the signing of the Russo-Chinese Treaty, in May, 1924, was the first preliminary step towards the Chinese revolution of the following year. For the United States and France protested publicly against the agreement and other Powers sabotaged it behind the scenes. Yet China defied them all in notes which were unusual in their vigor and independence. This was the initial throwing-down of the gauge of battle to the great nations of the west against whom China had rarely if ever raised her voice on an important issue.

Peking would never have dared such effrontery had it not been for the feeling that Russia stood behind her. But Russia was not enough. Japan is a powerful and wilful neighbour. Had Nippon sided with the Powers,

China would have hesitated before antagonising England, America, France, and other European states. But Japan was no longer the Japan of the twenty-one points; the bully and terror of a prostrate China. Events had taught the Mikado's government that it could not put its trust in the west and that it would not always be the better part of wisdom to embitter the great Asiatic republic of 400 million souls.

In China there were signs of an awakening of national consciousness. In Japan the rising tide of liberalism forced itself even upon the attention of that water-tight hierarchy which rules from Tokio. Moreover, much had happened to disillusion Nippon and to open its eyes as to the true heart of the Powers. First there had been the Washington Conference (November 12, 1921, to February 6, 1922), where Japan had learned that she could expect no true friendship from the United States. This impression was strengthened when, shortly afterwards, Great Britain succumbed to American pressure and abrogated her alliance with Japan. If a more stinging blow were needed it was furnished by the United States Anti-Japanese Immigration Law which aroused so much resentment in the island empire and was perhaps the most potent influence in weaning Japan from her western orientation and in changing her attitude towards China.

To be sure, Japan's financial position and her rôle as a world Power prevent her from cutting loose from the west altogether even if she wished. Furthermore, very powerful imperialistic and military elements still have an undeniable grip on the machinery of state at

Tokio, and Japan's aggressive attitude towards China cannot, therefore, disappear overnight. Nevertheless, the renunciation by Japan of her extra-territorial rights in China and the elevation of her minister in Peking to the rank of ambassador are definite signs of a new policy.

Though it may sound strange, it is nevertheless a fact that the relation to China of the world Powers who have a stake in her must affect their relations with Russia. It is true of England, to a greater extent of the United States, and to an extremely large extent of Japan.

"The real significance of a rapprochement between Russia and Japan," writes Yusuke Tsurumi, formerly of the Tokio Foreign Office and now a prominent leader of the Seiyukai Liberal Party,[1] "does not lie, as some people would think, in Japan's finding a position in a new alignment of world powers, as in her ultimate relationship with China. Japan's vital issue in foreign affairs is China. Japan's Russian policy is important in the degree that Russia affects China."

This is clear; China is the common ground on which Russia and Japan can meet. China is the issue on which Russia and Japan are most likely to quarrel, if they ever do.

Here, then, is the natural basis for the much-discussed Far Eastern bloc or "Triple Alliance" between Soviet Russia, Japan, and China. Moscow, it is understood, is categorically averse to entering into any alliances or ententes with bourgeois states. But it has

[1] American *Foreign Affairs*, December, 1924.

no objection to mutual cooperation with one or more of these when and as long as this lies in her own interests and advances the causes for which the Bolshevik government stands.

A well-known school of Japanese politicians is favourably disposed towards a bloc with Russia and China, and always advocated a rapprochement with the Communists for this and other reasons. Viscount Goto is the most prominent exponent of this group. In Soviet Russia, too, there are now not a few leaders who are inclined to follow a similar course. Yet it was not always so. During 1921, 1922 and 1923 the atmosphere was charged with antagonism to Japan, explained, first, by the Mikado's imperialistic policy in China and, second, by Japan's continued occupation of the northern Russian half of the island of Sakhalien which is rich in oil resources. During this period the Bolsheviks courted the good-will of the United States. They were anxious for a rapprochement with America and for the Sino-Soviet-American "bloc" to which the resumption of relations might ultimately have led. Several Russian statesmen whom I interviewed in Moscow in the course of 1922 and 1923 indeed intimated that the state of affairs in the Far East was rather conducive to such a combination. Certainly an agreement with Washington must have appeared more desirable and nearer then than a settlement with Japan. Nippon's refusal to evacuate Northern Sakhalien effectively barred the way to even the opening of negotiations. Besides, Japan had not yet received the drubbing at the hands of the United States which history had in store for her and the events which ultimately threw Japan into the arms of Russia had not yet occurred. Nor had Japan ceased to be the unscrupulous assailant of China's rights.

The United States, on the other hand, was pursuing a liberal policy towards China. People spoke of America as a friend of China. And Japan was an enemy of Russia. These two circumstances might well have given the diplomats in Moscow and Washington an opportunity of effecting an understanding between their countries. The granting of a Soviet concession to the Sinclair Exploration Company for the petroleum resources of Northern Sakhalien was without a doubt the Russian bid for such an understanding. Here was Moscow telling a big American concern with considerable political influence to go in and get the island's oil. Here was Soviet Russia offering an American company two ports on the eastern coast of upper Sakhalien right under the nose of Japan—ports where, if the necessity arose, ships flying the United States flag could coal and "oil". Obviously the Soviets expected that the American government would be ready and pleased to force the Japanese to leave the Russian part of Sakhalien. Obviously, too, the Bolsheviks believed that the United States would be glad to align Russia on its side in the Far Eastern struggle for a balance of power. Russia plays a decisive rôle on the Pacific. So does the United States. But the weakness of America's position in Asia is her distance from it. And the Philippines, exposed as they are, only add to this weakness. Under these conditions, a proffer of friendship from Russia, which would, incidentally, have opened Siberia's vast wealth to American capital, should have been welcome to Washington. Properly handled, the diplomatic situation created by the granting of the Sinclair concession would have given the United States a strong support in Asia and prevented the present Russo-Japanese "bloc" which, however imperfect now, may some day react to the detriment of American interests. Mr. Hughes, unfortunately, muffed the opportunity partly because of his provincialism, partly because he pursued a foolish Far Eastern policy which ultimately alienated China and Japan as well as Russia, and partly because the important consideration in all Russian affairs was to him the interests of the Standard Oil in the Caucasus. He may have been prepared to demand the evacuation of Sakhalien. He may have been prepared half-heartedly to support the Sinclair Company. But to take the next logical step and recognise the Soviet republic— that he really could not do until the Standard Oil's claim on Baku had been satisfied. Every American oil company is dear to the heart of the State Department, but the Standard has first call on its affections.

Nippon's troops occupied Northern Sakhalien in July, 1920, on the pretext of the alleged Nikolaiev massacre. Regardless of this circumstance, or perhaps because of it, the Soviet authorities leased the oil resources of the upper half of the island to Sinclair. There were thus four countries and one private party interested in Sakhalien petroleum: Russia, which owned the petroleum, Japan which wanted it, Great Britain, which upheld a rather flimsy claim to it of the Royal Dutch-Shell; Harry F. Sinclair, who had a concession for it, and the United States.

The preliminary concession was granted to Sinclair by the Far Eastern (Chita) Republic on May 14, 1921. It was ratified by the Chita authorities on January 7, 1922. When the Far Eastern Republic joined the Soviet Union, the agreement was confirmed by Moscow on January 26, 1923, and, finally, on August 16, 1923, Mr. Templeton and officials of the Bolshevik government affixed their signatures to the approved draft of the concession.

The concession gave Sinclair temporary monopoly rights, and permitted him to construct two ports on the eastern shore of the island. It was implicitly conditioned on United States recognition of Soviet Russia within five years, that is, by 1927.

Now Sakhalien, though an island, is really part of Siberia. In the six or seven months of winter it can be reached from the mainland on an ice sleigh. Moreover, it controls the mouth of the Amur River, which drains a large and tremendously rich section of the maritime provinces of Siberia.

It has been America's traditional policy to try to keep Japan off the Asiatic mainland. Hence President Wilson's efforts at Versailles to dislodge the Japanese from Shantung. Hence America's opposition to armed intervention in Siberia during the war,[2] and hence Mr.

---

[2] The idea of sending troops to Siberia occurred to the Japanese government soon after the United States entered the World War. In January, 1918, several Nipponese cruisers approached Vladivostok and one anchored in the harbour for the

Hughes' insistence on the evacuation of Russian Sakhalien.

On May 31, 1921, Mr. Hughes protested to the Mikado's government that the United States "could neither now nor hereafter recognise as valid any claims and titles arising out of the present occupation and control" of Northern Sakhalien. He reiterated these sentiments during the Washington Disarmament Conference. At the sixth plenary session of the conference (February 4, 1922), a statement by Baron Shidehara, then Japanese minister to Washington and a member of the Japanese delegation, was read in which Japan promised that "the military occupation of the

ostensible purpose of "protecting Japanese residents in the city". This was a tiny preliminary. In February, Japan was begging the Allies for permission to land forces on Siberian territory. On March 5th, a news message stated that "the British, French, and Italian ambassadors in Tokio intended yesterday or today jointly to ask Japan to safeguard Allied interests in Siberia". Nevertheless, Japanese intervention did not take place because the State Department objected. During the next few months, while Japan waited impatiently for the order to embark her soldiery, much pressure was put on President Wilson to consent to military intervention in Siberia. Soon it became evident that the Allies intended entering Siberia, no matter what decision Wilson arrived at. The question then confronting the President was: Shall the United States participate in the expedition? On August 3, 1918, the State Department finally decided in the affirmative but the document which contained the announcement of the decision was frank and highly undiplomatic in the way it cast suspicion on Japan's true motives. "Such military intervention," the communique read, ". . . would . . . be more likely to turn out to be a method of making use of Russia rather than to be a method of serving her." After America's consent had been forthcoming it was agreed that each Power send 7,000 men into Siberia. By some mistake, according to Prof. E. A. Ross of Wisconsin University, the United States despatched 8,500. "On the ground," he says, "that Japan was no longer bound by the agreement," the war party, then in the ascendancy in Tokio, sent in 73,400. Secretary of State Colby vehemently protested to Japan against this measure.

Russian province of Sakhalien is only a temporary measure, and will naturally come to an end as soon as a satisfactory settlement of the question shall have been arranged with an orderly Russian government." [3]

In response the American delegates "regretted that Japan should deem necessary the occupation of Russian territory as a means of assuring a suitable adjustment with a future Russian government." Furthermore, the Americans interpreted the Japanese assurances as meaning that "Japan does not seek . . . to set up an exclusive exploitation . . . of the resources of Sakhalien. . . ." Then, in conclusion, the United States statesmen firmly "reiterate the hope that Japan will find it possible to carry out within the near future her expressed intention of terminating finally the Siberian expedition and of restoring Sakhalien to the Russian people."

It was quite clear to all, however, that Japan had no intention of surrendering Sakhalien, her public pronouncements and Mr. Hughes' pious wishes notwithstanding. Tokio was then in no mood to deliver up the island's valuable oil- and coal-fields which she then controlled. The Japanese regarded these as excellent objects of exchange in a future settlement with Russia. The practical statesmen of the island empire saw no reason why they should voluntarily resign this advantage simply because Mr. Hughes had declared that he would enjoy seeing them do so. At Washington, the Japanese were obviously temporising. They announced

---

[3] *Official Minutes of the Washington Disarmament Conference,* pp. 346-354, Government Printing Office, Washington, D. C.

their intention of "sitting tight" in Sakhalien until what they would consider an "orderly" government had been established, nevertheless the State Department contented itself with the polite expression of a "hope" that Sakhalien would be evacuated. But when the United States was serious about opening the "closed door" to the petroleum resources of Mesopotamia for the Standard Oil it soon discovered how pressure could be brought to bear on England.

For many months the situation remained unchanged. Sinclair had a concession but could not work it because the Japanese were doing so without a concession and without permission from the Soviet government. Repeated attempts by the Moscow authorities to negotiate an agreement with the Japanese ended in failure. The Darien conference of 1922 was productive of no positive results nor were the efforts of Joffe, the Russian envoy, in 1923.

Meanwhile, events in China were crystallising for the revolution of 1924. At the same time public opinion in Japan, stimulated by groups which had trade, fishing and lumbering interests in Siberia, clamoured for the cessation of the Sakhalien occupation. By this time everyone was convinced that the Russian half of the island would not become a Jap dependency, and that Japanese control of it was but temporary. The realisation of this truth paved the way to the conversations in 1924 between Karakhan, the Soviet ambassador in Peking, and Yoshizava, the Japanese envoy in Peking.

On May 14, 1924, the Sino-Soviet Treaty was signed by Karakhan, and by Dr. Wang for the Chinese government. Everybody accepted it as the first step to a Russo-Japanese agreement. Nevertheless, Karakhan and Yoshizava wrestled with their problem for many months. Soon the Japanese agreed, in principle, to evacuate Northern Sakhalien. And now the question resolved itself down to the price which the Bolsheviks were ready to pay for the evacuation, or rather to the extent of the concessions which the Japanese could extort for it. The Tokio politicians were quite cynical about the matter. They had no desire to clothe themselves in a mantle of high-sounding phrases. They frankly admitted that they wanted the oil before they ordered their troops out.

For Russia the problem was complicated by the Sinclair concession. In their desire to satisfy all parties concerned, the Bolsheviks accordingly proposed a tripartite arrangement which would include Russia, Japan and Sinclair. This suggestion was first publicly made in an editorial of the Moscow *Isvestia*, the official organ of the Soviet government, and subsequently discussed by officials of the Commissariat of Foreign Affairs. Karakhan likewise placed it before Yoshizava in Peking. When Mr. Veatch, the vice-president of the Sinclair firm, arrived in Moscow in the summer of 1924 he stoutly denied any knowledge of a tri-partite proposal, and on being advised to consult the *Isvestia* editorial he insisted that it did not express the views of the government. Nevertheless, it is a fact, he was then already reconciled to it as the best possible solution of the problem and urged the Soviet government through the various officials whom he met, among them Minckin of the Chief Concessions Committee, to attempt to persuade the Japanese to accept it.

The Japanese, however, would have none of it. And naturally. They attached political as well as economic significance to Sakhalien oil and therefore refused to share it with an American company. As against the tri-partite arrangement of the Russians they put forward the following terms: A monopoly concession for ninety-nine years; Russia was to receive 5 per cent. of the oil produced; the Soviet labor laws were to remain in abeyance in Soviet Sakhalien.

Karakhan flatly declined to consider such an offer. Another break in the negotiations. Again Yoshizava went to Tokio for instructions. This was the situation late in the summer of 1924. It seemed as if the Japanese were "sparring for time", that they wished to draw out the negotiations until cold weather would make evacuation impossible till spring. They were gambling on unfavourable developments in the international position of the Soviet State which would enable them to strike a better bargain. But such developments did not materialise; in fact, the announcement in January, 1925, of the resignation of the American Secretary of State Hughes even strengthened the Russians, for the exit of Hughes was generally, though mistakenly, interpreted as increasing the probability of United States recognition of the Moscow government. On January 21, 1925, therefore, the Russo-Japanese Treaty was signed in Peking in the bedroom of the Japanese envoy, Yoshizava.

The treaty declares that "Japan shall effect the

military evacuation of Northern Sakhalien as promptly as climatic conditions permit," and in the following terms provides for the Japanese oil concession:

"The two contracting parties agree to conclude the agreement with regard to concessions within five months of the ratification of the treaty under the following terms:

"The Soviet government shall grant to parties of exploiters to be nominated by the Japanese government a concession amounting to 50 per cent. of the oil-fields in Northern Sakhalien, as described in the memorandum presented by the Japanese delegate on August 2nd.

"Each oil-field, so granted in concession, shall be rectangular in superfices, the area of each superfice not to exceed from 15 to 40 'dessiatin' and one area not to be situated near another.

"Should the Soviet government grant concessions regarding the remaining 50 per cent. of the oil-fields to a third party, the Japanese government shall be accorded equal opportunities.

"Besides the aforementioned concessions, the Soviet government shall grant to parties of exploiters to be nominated by the Japanese government the right of exploitation of the oil-fields for a term of from five to ten years, within an area of 1,000 Russian square miles on the east coast of Northern Sakhalien. The exploiters may begin the work of exploitation within one year after the agreement is concluded, and 50 per cent. of the output of the oil-fields shall belong to the afore-mentioned exploiters.

"The term of the concessions regarding both oil and coal shall be for a period of from forty to fifty years.

"Payments for the concessions to be made by the exploiters to the Soviet government will amount to from 5 to 15 per cent. of the total output of the oil-fields and from 5 to 8 per cent. of the total output of coal mines, and 45 per cent. of the output of the oil-gushers."

There can be no two opinions on the importance to Japan of the petroleum concession adumbrated in the treaty. The Mikado's island empire produces on the average of two million barrels of oil annually which covers only one-third of the domestic needs of the country. The other two-thirds has hitherto been imported from California—a procedure which has its obvious political disadvantages—and from the Dutch East Indies, and from Persia. Attempts to obtain concessions in Mexico and the Indies, and more recent efforts in Roumania and North Persia have been shattered on the opposition of governments and the obstruction of the powerful oil trusts.

The situation, especially in view of the steadily increasing demand for oil in Japan, has been an object of much concern to the authorities. It seems, however, that there is very little hope of raising the domestic output.

"Although the Japanese have been active in the working and developing of fields in the islands of Hondo, Hokaido, Taiwan (Formosa) and (southern) Sakhalien," says the report of the Federal Trade Commission on Foreign Ownership in the Petroleum Industry

(February, 1923), "the industry is said to be showing no progress, due to declines in production and the failure of attempts to develop new fields." [4]

Japan needs fuel for her growing industries and her large navy. She will now obtain it from Sakhalien. Northern Sakhalien has an area of approximately 16,280 square miles of which the greater part is probably petroliferous. The two large fields already known are situated (1) on the west coast opposite the mouth of the Amur River and (2) the richer, on the east coast between the Oka and Liangeri Rivers, a distance of some 220 miles. Oil was first discovered in 1870 and projecting was carried out by Sotoff in 1888 but no attempt was ever made at economic exploitation until the Japanese occupation.[5]

The Soviet-Japanese treaty stipulated the evacuation of Northern Sakhalien (the southern part, which comprises two-fifths of the whole, had been ceded to Japan as a result of the Russo-Japanese War), and the granting of an oil, as well as a coal, concession to a Japanese company. In accordance with the plan, and

---

[4] The *Japan Year Book* for 1924-25 says (p. 543): "The consumption of petroleum in Japan by private users is estimated in the neighbourhood of 2,600 koku [1 ton equals 6 koku] per annum. The total must reach some 5,000,000 koku if the consumption of the navy is taken into account. Against this the home supply in 1921 amounted to 1,516,000 or about 60 per cent. of the private consumption (and 30 per cent. of the total consumption). The shortage comes from California, Java, Borneo, and Mexico. The prospect of the industry is by no means reassuring; on the contrary, judging from the result of working in recent years, the fear is entertained that the limit of economic working may have been reached and that the hidden reservoirs are rapidly exhausting."

[5] According to one report the Japanese sank forty wells during the occupation.

as soon as weather permitted, the Japanese forces disembarked from the island (April, 1925), and thereupon the Bolshevik civil authorities arrived to assume their functions.

The signing of the concession adumbrated in the treaty was, needless to say, a more involved matter. First, the Sinclair contract was annulled, and then there followed several months of difficult negotiations with Japanese officials and industrialists who came to Moscow for the purpose.

The signing of the Russo-Japanese treaty which stipulated the oil concession caused considerable anxiety in the United States both on account of its political significance for the future of Far Eastern politics in which America is so vitally concerned, and also because the Sinclair concession was affected. It was charged generally that the Sinclair concession was voided in order to make possible the granting of the oil-field to a Japanese concern. This sounds plausible yet is not quite true for, as we shall see, there is room in Sakhalien for Sinclair and the Japanese. Moreover, the preliminary notice of the cancellation of the Sinclair lease was given to the company some seven months before the Russo-Japanese treaty was finally negotiated and when no one could foresee that Karakhan and Yoshizava would come to an agreement so soon. Sinclair was evicted from Sakhalien because he had not lived up to the terms of his contract. To be sure, the fact that Sinclair, as an American, was distasteful to Nippon played a rôle in the episode, but from the strict as well as from the liberally interpreted legal standpoint, the Soviet government was fully justified in terminating the understanding with Sinclair, and when in January, 1925, I asked Minckin, the secretary of the Chief Concessions Committee, what the Bolsheviks would do if Sinclair inspired a campaign against them in the United States, based on the allegation that "the Soviets have broken their pledge", he replied very simply, "We will publish the concession contract."

The Soviet government insisted that Sinclair had defaulted, and the courts sustained its argument.

Article II of the Sinclair concession contract made it incumbent upon the concessionaire to commence explorations between January 7, 1923, and January 7, 1924. Sixty days after the latter date he was to submit to the government a map indicating the scope and results of these efforts. This the Sinclair Company did not do. In accordance with the contract, the Soviet government allowed the company six months grace, but even at the end of these, operations had not commenced.

The Sinclair organisation did not deny these facts. But at the trial before the Moscow Provincial Court which took place on March 21, 22, 23 and 24, 1925, its attorneys argued that the company had been prevented from fulfilling the terms of the contract by "force majeure". The "force majeure" was the Japanese occupation. In the winter of 1924, Sinclair sent two American engineers, J. P. McCullough and L. F. MacLaughlin, to explore the concession area. These men travelled from the city of Vladivostok to the mouth of the Amur River in the worst part of the Arctic winter and then crossed the Strait from Siberia to Sakhalien on ice sleds. When they arrived the Japanese commandant arrested them, and placed them in a pen with the coolies who had been imported to labour for the oil exploiters. Later he released them and even dined with them. But the two engineers were permitted no liberty of movement. Soon they were politely deported. Under these circumstances, it was of course impossible for Sinclair to conduct any explorations. This assuredly, submitted the lawyers for the American Company, was "force majeure".

The Soviet government denied that it was. It argued thus: When Sinclair accepted the concession, he knew that the Japanese were in occupation of the oilfield which he pledged himself to explore. He knew, furthermore, that the Moscow government was neither able nor anxious to go to war in order to drive out the Japanese. He understood that it was for him to create conditions which would enable him to comply with the terms of the concession contract.

The fact of the Japanese occupation was neither ignored nor overlooked in the several contracts between the Sinclair Company and the Chita and Soviet governments. In fact, the supplementary lease of January 7, 1922, definitely takes account of it. Soviet spokesmen intimated on numerous occasions that it was largely because of the Japanese occupation and because of the Russian hope that through Sinclair's political influence in America it could be suspended, that the concession was granted to the American firm.

"At the time when it was concluded," reads an article

in the official Moscow *Pravda*, of February 27, 1925, "the Sinclair concession was undoubtedly of a partial political character. Paragraph 1 of the agreement grants the Soviet government the right to annul the contract in case any action on the part of the government of the United States should convince it that the American authorities would refuse to assist in putting the concession contract into practice. By concluding the agreement the Sinclair Company made the realisation of the agreement dependent upon the definite policy of the United States. From the point of view of both signees, the effectual carrying out of the lease was possible only on condition of the definite cooperation of America. Such definite cooperation and policy on the part of the United States, however, did not develop. Despite the fact that the Soviet government through Karakhan its ambassador in Peking, and, in a special note by Chicherin to the Japanese government, made every effort, as Templeton himself admitted, to aid the small preliminary Sinclair expedition to Sakhalien, and exerted itself to the utmost to enable the company to carry on its activities, the government of the United States made not the slightest move to facilitate the work of the company."

The author of the article refuses to accept as serious a statement made by Mr. Veatch, which characterises the relations between Russia and the United States as "friendly".

"It is not our fault," he then continues, "that the American government is the 'last of the Mohicans' among the nations which have recognised the Soviet

Union. Nor is it our fault that the capitalists of the Sinclair company could not prevail upon their government to give them the cooperation necessary to the execution of the concession contract."

It is clear from this summary of the situation, as it would be from numerous similar pronouncements by Soviet leaders and in the Soviet press, that the undisguised purpose of the granting of the Sakhalien concession to Sinclair was that of thus persuading Washington to use its "good offices" with the Tokio government to effect the evacuation of the Russian half of the island. The Sinclair organisation was well aware of this and, fully conscious, gladly assented to playing the rôle of common denominator for the United States and the Soviet governments. Had the State Department succeeded in convincing the Mikado's statesmen of the seriousness of its demand for Japanese evacuation of Sakhalien, or had it given the least indication of good-will to Moscow, the Sinclair concession may never have been scrapped, and the Russo-Japanese Treaty, inevitable in any case, would not have contained as one of its most important terms the outline of a Sakhalien oil concession to a Japanese syndicate. Moreover, it is quite conceivable that in such an event, America's political and economic position in the Far East, especially in China, would now be much stronger than it is.

When the Moscow Provincial Court ruled the Sinclair concession null and void, the Company on May 22, 1925, appealed the case to the Soviet Supreme Court which sustained the decision of the lower court.

Students of the protocols of both these trials must easily be convinced that the government was well within its rights in pleading for the cancellation of the agreement and that Sinclair's legal position was absolutely indefensible. At the Court proceedings the several concession leases were examined in detail by the attorneys of the government as well as by those of the defence and it appears clearly from the arguments presented that the American Company broke many of the clauses which it had pledged itself to keep.

It is true that Robert Lansing, former United States Secretary of State, who had been retained by Sinclair, addressed a letter to the company on March 12, 1925, in which he disputed the Soviet right of annulment. Yet he admitted in the same communication that the concession contract obliged Sinclair to carry out one drilling operation before the end of the second contract year. This Sinclair had not done. All authorities agreed, of course, that the terms of the lease were infringed. There remained only the issue of "force majeure", and the Russian jurists ruled that a situation which had maintained at the moment of the signing of the contract could not properly be interpreted as "force majeure," especially when the agreement distinctly mentioned the occupation.

The Lansing letter was addressed to Mr. Veatch, the vice-president of the Sinclair Exploration Company, and is made public here for the first time. Mr. Lansing refers in his opening paragraph to the contracts, agreements and data which he has examined, and then proceeds as follows:

"From the examination of the above documents, I am clearly of the opinion that the suit brought to obtain the cancellation of the concession granted by the Soviet government to the Exploration Company for production of petroleum, *et cetera*, in Russian Sakhalien is entirely without foundation and should be dismissed by the Soviet court.

"The reasons for my opinion are briefly:

"That the concession agreements were entered into with the full knowledge of the parties; that the Japanese were at the time in military occupation of Russian Sakhalien and that presumably the occupation would be continued for a considerable time. The force clause (Art. 35, Agreement, Jan. 7th, 1922), was drawn precisely to cover this situation, for it provides for the contingency where 'the Company should be delayed in the beginning of the operations mentioned in this agreement' because of 'military activities' or an 'insurmountable force.' The use of such language, as well as the history of the concession, demonstrate that the possibility of delay in beginning operations because of the existing Japanese occupation of Russian Sakhalien was in the contemplation of the parties at the time the agreement was made. There is no limitation expressed or implied that the 'military activities' mentioned in Article 35 shall be such as are unforeseen or unexpected.

"That the deposit of 200,000 Russian gold roubles was accepted by the Soviet government with the full knowledge of the fact that the Japanese occupation of Russian Sakhalien might prevent the beginning of operations by the Company, and that it would be inequitable for the Government to take advantage of this fact to cancel the concession and retain this sum as forfeit.

"That, while the Company has the 'right' to carry on explorations for the named mineral substances, 'During the first five years of this concession the Company is *not obligated* to commence production of the mineral substances' (Art. 2, Agreement, Jan. 7th, 1922), and there is *no obligation* on the Company to do any exploration or any other work on the concession except 'to set up and put into operation one drilling outfit before the end of the second year (*i.e.*, Jan. 7th, 1925) and a second drilling outfit before the end of the fifth year of the concession' (Art. 23 ID). The company endeavoured in good faith to carry out this obligation but was forceably prevented from doing so by the Japanese Military authorities occupying Russian Sakhalien. The failure of the company was therefore due to *force majeure* as defined in Article 35 of the concession agreement. Moreover, there was *no obligation* on the Company in the course of the first year 'to commence exploration and research work' on the spot as alleged in a complaint of the Soviet government in the suit above mentioned. . . . [Lansing's italics throughout.]

"(Signed) ROBERT LANSING."

In August, 1925—four months after the evacuation of Sakhalien and three months after the cancellation of the Sinclair contract—negotiations opened in Moscow between the Chief Concessions Committee and the Japanese. For the purposes of these conversations, Adolph Joffe, former Soviet Minister in Peking and Russia's first delegate to several conferences with the Japanese, was appointed vice-chairman of the Chief Concessions Committee and delegated by the Bolshevik government to assume charge of the pourparlers. In July, Tanaka Tokichi, Nippon's ambassador to Soviet Russia, had arrived in Moscow accompanied by Lieutenant-General Nakazato, one-time Commandant of a Japanese naval base, who represented several Japanese petroleum companies, and Okumura Mazao, an important official of the Mitsuibushi Corporation, a mining and petrol company. These informed the Chief Concessions Committee that a Japanese Consortium had been formed with a capital of ten million yen to exploit the petroleum resources of Northern Sakhalien.

Definite discussions commenced on August 17th when the spokesmen of both parties made statements of general principle. The broad lines of the concession were, it will be remembered, defined by the Russo-Japanese treaty of January 21, 1925. Nevertheless, it required as many as five months to arrive at a mutual agreement on detailed terms.

Labour conditions on the concessions, and the royalty percentage which the Soviet government was to receive in return for the grant presented the most difficult problems. The Japanese had originally urged the absolute suspension of Soviet labour laws in Northern Sakhalien. But on this point the Bolsheviks were unable and unwilling to yield. Even if the Soviet statesmen were inclined to permit a fraction of the workers of the country to be robbed of the benefits of Communist labour legislation, they would never have dared to antagonise the proletarians of the land by so doing. Such a measure would have exposed them to the obvious accusation that they were delivering labourers over to foreign capitalists for merciless exploitation. From every point of view, it was impossible for Moscow to accede to this demand.

The Japanese further insisted on the right to import a limitless number of coolies from China and Japan. This question likewise presented considerable difficulty.

The third point at issue was that of the royalties which the Japanese concessionaire was to pay to the Soviet authorities in return for the right to exploit the Sakhalien oil resources.

Needless to say, the Russian, as well as the Japanese negotiators, were constantly in communication with their respective governments, and it may be said, without any fear of contradiction, that no step was taken and no decision made before the political organs in Moscow and Tokio were consulted. No attempt was made by either government to hide its interests and participation in the conversations, and it is characteristic that the Japanese ambassador, as well as the important members of his staff, were present at the signing ceremony of the concession.

After some four months of deliberations, during which serious breakdowns several times threatened, the contract was finally subscribed on December 14, 1925, by Felix Dzerzhinsky, Chairman of the Supreme Economic Council for the Soviet government, and by Admiral Nakasato, for the Associated Northern Sakhalien Petroleum Corporation. The oil concession, as well as the coal concession which was granted simultaneously, was countersigned by M. Litvinov, Assistant Commissar for Foreign Affairs.

The lease states explicitly that the Japanese Company shall be bound by all Soviet labour legislation now in force as well as by any regulations which may in the future be enacted. Trade Unions are recognised, and the principle of collective bargaining with them accepted as obligatory by the Japanese. The rules prevailing throughout Soviet Russia for the social insurance of workers, a minimum annual vacation of one fortnight and similar amenities will be binding upon the company. All this applies with equal force to the Russians and foreigners employed on the oil-fields.

Fifty per cent. of the administrative and technical personnel and of the highly skilled workers may be brought from abroad, but only 25 per cent. of the unskilled labourers are to be non-Russian. The Soviet government, moreover, reserves the right to reexamine these percentages every three years with a view to their reduction. The Bolsheviks saw the cogency of the Japanese argument that Sakhalien was an industrially undeveloped region, sparsely populated by people whose chief occupation was fishing, and that trained workers in sufficiently large numbers were unavailable in Eastern Siberia. Nevertheless, it was felt in Moscow that a permanent system of contract coolie labour was not in accordance with Bolshevik principles, and that the strict limitation of the number of imported workers and the gradual reduction even of this must be a *sine qua non* of the concession.   The entrepreneur undertakes to provide the employees with free living quarters, and with food at cost, the cost price being determined by the Soviet government.

The contract is for a period of forty-five years. Four thousand eight hundred dessiatines on the eastern coast of Northern Sakhalien are designated as petroliferous.   Of these, one-half is allocated to the Associated North Sakhalien Petroleum Corporation, and the other half retained by the Soviet government which may, if it so pleases, exploit the field itself or grant it to a second concessionaire.   The agreement stipulated further that another field in North Sakhalien approximately 1,000 square versts (440 square miles) in extent is to be explored by the corporation during the next ten years and then divided equally between the concessionaire and the Bolshevik State.

On a total annual oil production of 30,000 metric tons or less the Soviet government is to receive a royalty of 5 per cent.   For every additional 10,000 metric tons a royalty of 0.25 per cent. will be added until a yearly output of 430,000 tons is reached.   On this or a greater quantity 15 per cent. royalties will be paid.[6]   Money fees equal to 45 per cent. of the value of all gusher oil and a royalty on gas varying from 10 to 35 per cent., according to its gasoline content, are

[6] The Anglo-Persian Oil Co. is paying the Teheran government a royalty of 16 per cent.

likewise to be delivered to the Soviet Exchequer. In addition to these royalties, an annual rental of 4 per cent. is provided for.

The Corporation may export all its products, whether raw or refined, duty-free and without obtaining special permission. Similarly, there will be no tariff on whatever machinery, equipment, and raw materials the company may wish to import for its operations, or on any goods and food imported for distribution among its workers. The Japanese may build buildings, erect refineries, lay pipe-lines, and generally construct such facilities as will be necessary for the proper prosecution of their work. At the expiration of the term of the concession, or before it if for some reason the agreement lapses earlier, all these structures, as well as the entire equipment of the field, become the inalienable property of the Soviet government. The Japanese renounce every right to it.

Differences and disputes between the concessionaire and the concession granter are subject to the final jurisdiction of the Soviet Supreme Court.

The Soviets are more or less pleased with the terms of the concession, especially since it leaves in their hands approximately two-thirds of the known oil resources of the Russian half of the island. Writing on the Japanese concession in the Moscow *Trade and Industrial Gazette*, of December 15, 1925, M. Gurevitch, one of the Soviet experts who participated in the negotiations with the Japanese, says:

"Some time ago, when Sakhalien was occupied by Japan, we concluded a less satisfactory agreement than this with the American Sinclair Company in the hope that the latter, operating through its government, would succeed in liberating Northern Sakhalien. Sinclair, as we know, did not carry out his part of the agreement and as a result it was cancelled by our Supreme Court. We have now, through direct discussion with the Japanese government, succeeded in achieving the liberation of Northern Sakhalien on far more favourable terms. This was possible, thanks to our economic progress and to the strengthening of the international position of our Union."

The Japanese, it seems, were no less gratified by the contract. On December 15th, the Moscow daily *Economic Life*, organ of the Supreme Economic Council, published an interview with Admiral Nakasato, the representative of the Associated Northern Sakhalien Petroleum Company, in which he stated:

"We justly look upon the agreement just concluded as a guarantee of cordial relations between the Soviet Union and Japan, and we are fully convinced that the carrying out of the contract will be a means of establishing friendship between the two nations.

"Japan's petroleum requirements are growing day by day. The concession for the production of petroleum on Northern Sakhalien, which has been granted us by the government of the Soviet Union, will satisfy the present needs of the Japanese industrial system. The Eastern coast of Northern Sakhalien is at present a wilderness. We hope that our enterprises will effect the development of that region, and that we, on our part, will thus be enabled to participate in the general economic progress of the Soviet Union."

All parties are agreed that within three or four years, when work on the concession is well under way, Japan will no longer be forced to purchase oil from foreign trusts. Alike, the Japanese Navy and Nippon's industrial system will, in all probability, be adequately supplied with petroleum by the Northern Sakhalien fields. This, needless to say, is for Japan as important politically as it is economically. In the meantime, and while production on Sakhalien will not have attained a high level, Japan intends importing as much oil as possible from the Caucasus. Shortly after the signing of the Sakhalien concession, M. Sasaki, secretary of the Japanese Embassy in Moscow, undertook a visit to Odessa, Batum, and Baku for the purpose of investigating the possibility of oil exports to Japan. In an interview with the Moscow *Isvestia*, Mr. Sasaki explained that Japan was purchasing large quantities of oil in the United States and other countries but that these, even taken together with Japan's domestic yield, did not cover the nation's needs.

"Besides," Mr. Sasaki added, "American oil is too costly as it is transported over 5,000 miles. There fore, Sakhalien oil is of great importance to Japan, especially since the Japanese port of Hokkaido is only 400 miles from Sakhalien."

It appears, therefore, that whether or not a political alliance exists between Russia and Japan, a petroleum entente certainly has been established, for from every point of view, it is more advantageous to Japan to produce and buy her oil in Soviet Russia than in any other country of the world.

There can be no question as to the good faith of the Russians in concluding the agreement with the Japanese Corporation for the exploitation of the Northern Sakhalien fields. In the final analysis, however, the success of the undertaking depends on the good-will maintaining between the governments of the two countries. Both parties realise that the concession will be threatened the moment Soviet-Nipponese relations pass under a cloud. The Sakhalien contract is thus not merely an indication of a spirit of trust and friendship between the two great Far Eastern Powers, but also in a way, a guarantee against future trouble. And if difficulties do arise in other spheres, there will always be the voice of certain very powerful economic interests in Japan, whose concession will be at stake, to sound the call to caution. The oil of Sakhalien is calculated to quiet any stormy souls in Tokio. It is, without a doubt, an important component part of the mortar of the still imperfect Sino-Soviet-Japanese "bloc".

The Japanese, especially, make no secret of the political implications of the concession. Mr. Kshahava, one of the officials of the Associated Northern Sakhalien Petroleum Corporation, who assisted in the negotiating of the contract, did not, for instance, hesitate to connect the concession with the Chinese-Japanese-Russian "bloc" in an interview with the Moscow *Isvestia* (October 15, 1925). He emphasises Japan's need of Russian oil, coal, flax, salt, etc., and adds:

"Thus, Japan and the Soviet Union are greatly interested in the development of their economic relations with one another. This is the best stimulus for the formation by our countries, together with China, of a triple union which would play a decisive rôle in Far Eastern affairs. The establishment of such a trinity could not, of course, interfere with the various interests within the several nations. The realisation of this idea [of the triple bloc] is already quite possible at the present moment."

One Sakhalien oil problem remains unsolved: that of the petroliferous lands not assigned to the Associated North Sakhalien Petroleum Corporation. There is, at least, as much oil left for the Russians as has been leased to the Japanese. What will they do with it? They could farm out the second half of the oil field to some European or American concessionaire. They may rent it to the Japanese. Or they may exploit it themselves.

A concession to an American company—if one could be found to accept it—would encounter almost insurmountable political obstacles. A concession to a French or British firm would probably meet with similar objections in Japan. On the other hand, it would be questionable wisdom from the point of view of the Soviets to double the present acreage of the Japanese and thereby give them a virtual monopoly. Nevertheless, this is a possibility.

There are in the Soviet oil world a number of persons, among them G. Lomov, president of the Moscow Naphtha Syndicate, who would press for exploitation by the Bolsheviks. China is a great market where industries are developing, railroads multiplying and in which millions of kerosene lamps are used. If the Russians were producing petroleum in Sakhalien they could make a far more effective bid for the market of 400,000,000 inhabitants than they can at present. They would certainly have a handicap over the Standard Oil and Royal Dutch who now struggle for its control. But to produce oil in a new field one must have much free money. And that the Bolshevists have not.

The future of the non-Japanese section of the Sakhalien oil field is thus veiled in uncertainty. Much depends on how the Japanese Corporation proceeds. The Sakhalien concession frees Japan from dependence on the two great oil Powers of the world—the United States and Great Britain. These Powers are also the two great enemies of Japan—all their protestations to the contrary notwithstanding. If the Japanese Corporation will be guided by this realisation, its relations with the Soviet government should be smooth.

CHAPTER VIII

IN THE SHAHDOM OF PERSIA

WHILE the entire world thirsts for oil and hunts it
in every out-of-the-way corner of the earth, the rich
North Persian petroleum fields just across the sea
from Baku lie idle and await the exploiter. The
Standard Oil Company, the Anglo-Persian, Sinclair,
a French consortium, and, the Japanese, too, have all
made efforts to acquire rights to this liquid treasure
near the Caspian. Without avail, however, for the
Soviet government holds the much-sought key and still
refuses to relinquish it.

In the realm of oil, it is as important to control
resources as to own them. From this point of view,
the petroleum which lies beneath the surface of the
five northern provinces of the Shahdom of Persia may
really be added to the tremendous quantities in Russia.

Russia's strategic position with respect to North
Persian oil is in the first place geographical, in the
second political. A study of the map will show that
the five northern provinces (Azerbaijhan, Ghilan,
Mazandaran, Astrabad, and Khorosan) are only a
short, cheap boat ride from Baku, whereas more than
700 miles of difficult mountains and wide deserts separate them from the Persian Gulf. To lay a pipe-line
from the oil-fields to the gulf would probably be an
engineering feat the like of which has never yet been

successfully attempted, and, what with the distance and the necessity of pumping the liquid over long stretches of sharply-ascending slopes, the price of the product would prohibit production. Moreover, Persia has practically no railroads. Machines and other equipment could not be transported from the south except on the backs of half a million or more camels.

For all commercial purposes the only outlet from the North Persia fields to the world is via Baku, across the Caucasus to Batum and thence through the Dardanelles. Even could a pipe-line be laid to the Persian Gulf, the sea voyage from Bushire or any other Persian port to Europe would be many times longer than the one from the Black Sea. The freight item thus introduced would inevitably make for huge deficits. In other words, all imports required in the exploitation of the North Persian field and all its petroleum exports must be carried in transit through the Caucasus. Very likely part of the Persian product will be refined in the modern refineries at Baku, much of it will flow down the Baku-Batum pipe-line now in use and another on which construction is soon to commence. Finally, the Russian harbor of Batum would be the gate through which Persian petroleum would reach its markets.

It is clear, therefore, that alone the "lay of the land" gives Russia the power to veto any concession to the North Persian resources, for Moscow will assuredly not permit a concessionaire who is *persona non grata* to it to use Russian territory for transit purposes. This objective advantage lavished by the cruel forces of Nature which know no equality and for which the "survival of the fittest" is a most agreeable law, has now been approved and sanctioned by the hand and the mind of man. Enter politics.

The story opens in the "once upon a time" when a Czar still ruled in St. Petersburg. It was in March, 1916, that Akaky Mefodievitch Khostaria, a Georgian by birth and a Russian citizen, obtained from the Persian government the right to drill for oil in the five northern provinces. But it was obtained "under coercion by the late Czarist government and without the consent of the Medjhelis (parliament)".[1] The Czar's agents were in a position to exert such pressure

[1] This statement was contained in a letter from M. Dowleh printed in the London *Times* of December 26, 1921, in which the ex-minister wrote:

"The concession, as I have just stated, was granted to Mr. Khostaria by one of my predecessors in 1916, and when a year later I became Prime Minister, I actually did confirm it; but soon afterwards when I had resigned, the Russian Revolution broke out, and the Persian government, on the ground that this, together with other concessions, had been obtained under coercion by the late Czarist government and without the consent of the Persian National Assembly (Medjhelis) which at that time was not sitting, declared it to be invalid; and the Soviet government of Russia not only expressed their entire approval of the action of the Persian government, but were actually the first to suggest it, so that when in 1918, I once again became Prime Minister, the Russian, as well as the Persian government, considered this concession invalid, and therefore as already non-existent. . . ."

"Moreover," continues the ex-Premier, "his Britannic Majesty's Minister at Teheran, in accordance with instructions received from the British government, expressed himself in full agreement with the views of the Persian government in regard to this concession [it had then not yet been transferred to the Anglo-Persian Company] and in a letter addressed to me at that time, actually gave expression to this feeling. . . ."

"With regard to the concession having been originally obtained by coercion, or granted voluntarily by the Persian government to a Russian subject, I believe that taking in consideration the period when it was granted is in itself sufficient to enable a judgment to be formed."

as a result of Persia's unfortunate and dependent financial and political status. Persia, once the vast empire which reached "from India even unto Ethiopia", was in more recent times the helpless victim of the rivalries between two more modern world domains: Great Britain and monarchic Russia. For it was inevitable that Britain and Russia should come to grips in the Near East, in Persia, where the outposts of their empires met, and where the natural tendency of the former to expand northwards and of the latter to extend southwards clashed. England sought control in Persia in order to prevent Russia's further expansion into Central Asia, to protect India, the most precious jewel in her imperial diadem, against what were generally only imagined dangers, and finally to push towards the Caucasus. On the other hand, Russia desired a foothold in Persia for the purpose of keeping the British away from the Caucasus and of safeguarding her Central Asiatic possessions. Throughout decades the struggle raged until finally, in 1907, the two powers declared a truce in the East. England needed Russia's aid in checking Germany, which was already becoming a menace to the British lion. Russia was disturbed by Austro-Hungary's advances in the Balkans. Moreover, the Czar coveted Constantinople and the Straits. Such were the interests which paved the way for the formation of the Franco-Russo-British Entente against Germany, Austro-Hungary and Turkey. Under these circumstances it became imperative to compose the differences which made for friction between Russia and England in Asia. This was especially true in view of the fact that Russia was then too weak to continue the struggle against England or to remain without friends: Japan had bled her in the war of 1904–1905, while the revolutionary disturbances of 1905–1906, one of the worst centres of which was Baku, so shattered the inner defences of the empire that an armistice with the Czar's rival in Asia became an imperative necessity. Accordingly, the treaty of August 31, 1907, was signed in St. Petersburg by Sir Arthur Nicolson, His Majesty's Ambassador at the Czar's court, and by Isvolsky, then Russian foreign minister. It provided that both contracting parties were to keep "hands off" Tibet, that Russia was to recognise Great Britain's protectorate in Afghanistan, and that Persia was to be cut up into "spheres of influence". Russia took the northern part, bounded on the one side by her own border and the Caspian Sea and on the other by an arbitrary line "starting from Kasr-i-Shirin, passing Isfahan, Yezd, Kakhk, and ending at the point on the Persian frontier at the intersection of the Persian and Afghan frontiers". Below this was the neutral zone, and then, in the southeast—the British "sphere" which was coterminous with Baluchistan and Afghanistan. From 1907 to 1917 Persia was ruled by the terms of this division, a division made without the knowledge or consent of the Persian people.

The Czar kept his Cossacks in the north, marched them into Teheran at will when he desired to overthrow one of the Shah's cabinets or to drive Mr. Morgan Shuster, the American financial adviser of the Persian government, out of the country, and generally lorded

over the "sphere" which he had acquired by agreement
with England. It is not difficult to understand, therefore, how Russia could have coerced the Persian state
into granting Khostaria the concession for the North
Persian oil-fields. That was in 1916. A year later
Russia was overrun by revolution; soon the Bolsheviks were embroiled in a civil war which absorbed
all their energies; Russian influence in Persia was
reduced to nil, and the British, forgetting the
"spheres" arrangement, made themselves masters in
all of Persia and sent troops into the Caucasus in an
effort to detach that rich oil region from the rest of
Russia.

But it was not long before the Red Army was forcing its way down into the Caucasus and even extending
a finger towards the British military base in North
Persia. Khostaria, who knew well that the Communists
would view his Czarist concession with rather un-
friendly eyes, hastily, and very wisely, sold his claim
on May 8, 1920, to the Anglo-Persian Company in consideration of 100,000 pounds. (Subsequently, it is
said, he received additional 225,000 pounds from the
same organisation.)

The Anglo-Persian Company must have assumed
that it would be years before Russia was sufficiently
recuperated to resume her rôle as an important factor
in the life of Persia. Therefore it felt safe in acquiring
the Khostaria rights. But the calculation was wrong.
On February 26, 1921, the Soviet government signed
a treaty with the Persian government, and in April,
Theodore A. Rothstein, the first Communist envoy to

Persia, made his entry into Teheran. By the terms of
the treaty Russia voluntarily renounced and returned
to Persia all concessions and unusual rights which the
Czar's government had extracted from the Persian
state. The same article (No. 13) provided that none
of these returned concessions might be regranted to a
foreign citizen or company without the consent of the
Soviet.

The Khostaria concession was thus automatically
annulled. *Ipso facto*, the rights which the Anglo-
Persian had purchased from Khostaria were annulled.
In Persia this development produced much joy. For
the Anglo-Persian's valuable oil concessions of 1901 in
South Persia already gave that company, and through
it the British government, a tremendous influence upon
the finances, politics and inner peace of the country.
A further concession in the north would make Persia
the prostrate vassal of Downing Street. It would,
moreover, have antagonised the new, revolutionary
Russia, which had won great sympathy in Persia by
its championing of the rights of the oppressed peoples
of the East and by its advocacy of a strong, unified
Persia which could resist British pressure.

The Anglo-Persian, however, did not accept the word
of the Persian government as final. At an annual
meeting of the company, Sir Charles Greenway, its
president, expressed his "profound astonishment" at
the action of the Persian government and still doubted
whether "the Persian government will deliberately commit their country to so suicidal a policy" as that of
repudiating the Anglo-Persian's claim, of which Persia

had never approved, or the Khostaria concession, which the Medjhelis had never confirmed.

The Anglo-Persian and the British Foreign Office [2] argued that Khostaria had become a Georgian subject and denied the Soviet government's suzerainty in Georgia.

The Persian statesmen, on the other hand, considered this a closed chapter and entered into negotiations with the Standard Oil Company. These met with success, and early in 1921 the Medjhelis instructed the Persian government to grant the Rockefeller firm a lease, on certain terms and with certain provisions,[3] to the North Persian petroleum deposits for a fifty-year period. "By doing so the Persian government committed an error," writes Ambassador Rothstein, "in that it failed to comprehend the meaning of the 13th article of the Russo-Persian treaty, which prohibits the transfer of our former concession to citizens of a third power without our [Russia's] consent." [4] This was the essence of the protest which Rothstein lodged with the Teheran Foreign Office on November 23, 1921.

Nor was the Anglo-Persian Company slow in making its objections vocal. Having bought out Khostaria, it

[2] *New Age,* London, January, 1923.

[3] On November 14, 1921, the Persian Legation in London issued a statement on the North Persian concession which read, in part, as follows: "Lately a concession has been approved by the Persian Parliament to be granted to the American Standard Oil Company concerning the oil-fields of North Persia, one of the principal clauses of this concession being that the said company is precluded from transferring to or associating with any other company without the consent of the Persian Parliament." (*Times,* November 15, 1921.)

[4] Introduction to Russian translation of *War for Persian and Mesopotamian Oil,* by E. Schultze.

insisted that the concession was its own and that the Standard Oil therefore had no right to accept a conflicting lease. The Standard had thus aroused the ire not only of its traditional business rival, the Anglo-Persian, but, also, directly of the British government, which holds a majority of the company's shares. These developments served merely to darken the already heavy clouds which at that time hung over the diplomatic relations between the United States and Great Britain. Oil had caused the storm. The trouble dated back to April 24, 1920, when the San Remo Petroleum agreement was arrived at between Great Britain and France. Signed by Sir John Cadman for England and Philip Berthelot for France, and approved by Lloyd George and Millerand, it divided the oil of Mesopotamia between the two countries and virtually excluded the United States.

To the American oil interests this was a matter of no small importance. It meant that they had been barred from one of the world's potentially richest petroleum deposits. Accordingly the atmosphere grew charged with electricity, and angry notes flew across the Atlantic from the State Department to Downing Street, and from Downing Street to the State Department. President Wilson had protested against the Anglo-French partition of Iraq oil on March 4, 1920, even before the San Remo memorandum had been subscribed to but when the problem with which it dealt had come up for discussion. On May 13, 1920, John W. Davis, United States Ambassador in London, "pursuant to the instructions" of his government, delivered a note to Earl Curzon regarding the "unfortunate impression in the minds of the American public, that the authorities of His Majesty's government in the occupied region (Palestine and Iraq) had given advantage to British oil interests which were not accorded to American companies, and further that Great Britain had been preparing quietly for exclusive control of the oil resources of this region." [5]

Before Curzon could reply, the San Remo agreement was published by the press (July 20), and promptly Mr. Davis addressed another note to the British Foreign Office in which he warned that this agreement between the British and French governments "will result in a grave infringement of the mandate principle," [6] the principle by virtue of which Palestine and Mesopotamia have become British Crown colonies in fact if not in name. Curzon of Kedleston replied on August 9th. He abandoned not an inch of the British position. On the contrary, he insisted that "the suggestion that Great Britain, during the period of military occupation of the mandated territories, has been preparing for exclusive control of their oil resources is . . . devoid of foundation. . . . " Moreover, he stated very plainly that since the United States was not a member of the League of Nations she had no business interfering in the mandate question. Indeed,

[5] Correspondence between His Majesty's government and the United States Ambassador respecting Economic Rights in Mandated Territories. *White Paper of the British government* (Cmd. 1226), 1921.

[6] Correspondence between His Majesty's government and the United States Ambassador respecting Economic Rights in Mandated Territories. *White Paper of the British government* (Cmd. 1226), 1921.

the note contained some very irritating charges against the irregularities of American oil policy in Haiti and Costa Rica, charges which Secretary of State Colby's reply note dated November 20th "does not attempt to refute". Mr. Colby's epistle insisted that the "United States as a participant in that conflict [the World War] and as a contributor to its successful issue . . . can not consider itself debarred from the discussion of any of its consequences, or from participation in the rights and privileges secured under the mandates provided for in the Treaties of Peace." [7]

This thesis the British government continued to dispute "politely but firmly". Meanwhile critical months passed. England felt that her entire imperial policy in the East was being interfered with; the Arab tribes in Iraq were growing restive and gave the British much cause for anxiety; the Zionists gritted their teeth at the continual delays in the ratification of the mandate which was to confirm their theoretical political rights in Palestine; Great Britain was prevented from consolidating her war gains in the Near East. She desired the League to approve the mandates, but neither England nor the other members of the League of Nations could get themselves to make a step which would anger America. Washington, on the other hand, refused to yield.

Seeking a solution, Sir John Cadman was sent to the United States. During the war Cadman had been Inter-Allied Oil Director. Later he was chief of the Petroleum Executive of the British government. He

[7] Curzon note of February 28, 1921. See *White Paper*.

had drafted and signed the San Remo Agreement. Moreover, he was an official of the Anglo-Persian Company. Sir John's visit to America was considered "to be a move by the British government to come to an understanding with the State Department on its world oil policy." [8]

The atmosphere in America was none too conducive to the success of Sir John's mission. The State Department and the Standard Oil were of the same mind in the matter, and the one gave moral encouragement to the other. On November 17, 1920, on the eve of the Englishman's arrival in New York, W. C. Teagle, president of the Standard Oil Company, saw fit to address the Washington meeting of the American Petroleum Institute in this wise:

"Our British friends, in endeavouring to explain the position their government has taken since the armistice, have argued that if the United States is now supplying 70 per cent. of the world's [oil] production, we should be content with things as they are. This is an entirely fallacious view. Is it reasonable to ask that Americans go heedlessly on to the quick exhaustion of their own supply and then retire from the oil business? The American petroleum industry cannot accept such a conclusion. It must look to the development of petroleum outside the United States." [9]

Mr. Teagle then proceeded to a frank discussion of the San Remo agreement in which connection he

[8] Despatch from London to *The Public Ledger* by Carl W. Ackerman, dated December 6, 1920.
[9] New York *Times*, November 18, 1920.

warned that the United States "might be forced as a matter of necessary self-protection to consider the adoption of measures reciprocally to consider its petroleum resources for its own people and stop the supply to other nations." This was a broad hint that America was prepared to declare an oil blockade against England and bar English companies from producing in United States fields.

Faithful politicians took the Standard Oil cue and carried the debate to the floor of the United States Senate. On January 6, 1921, Senator McKellar explained that "if Great Britain is not permitted to get oil from this country her navy will be severely handicapped, and many ships of her mercantile marine will be put out of commission. She will be obliged to come to terms." [10] Senator, now Secretary of State, Kellogg then suggested that "the government should by treaty provide for the protection of American interests in the development of oil lands in foreign countries," and spoke of "retaliatory legislation if Great Britain refuses the square deal to Americans." [11] Senator Phelan of California spoke in a similar vein; the Standard Oil had many supporters.

In the meantime Sir John Cadman had returned to England, his mission a failure. On arriving home his statements to the correspondents were extremely pessimistic. He characterised the situation as dangerous. And he was not alone in this view. One has merely to peruse the British and American press of this period

[10] Paris edition New York *Herald,* January 8, 1921.
[11] Editorial *The New York Times,* January 8, 1921.

to see how aroused the public temper was and how hostile the relations between the two nations had become. Serious journals even discussed the possibility of an Anglo-American war.

When the Republican Mr. Hughes succeeded the Democratic Mr. Colby on March 4, 1921, he took up the battle where his predecessor had left it, for oil politics stands above parties. The torrent of notes continued. Lord Curzon's reply of March 6th was considered "conciliatory in tone", nevertheless it rejected the American contentions. So the trouble dragged on to a seemingly interminable end. Diplomacy appeared to be powerless in the face of the crisis.

Early in 1921, it will be remembered, the Standard Oil had been granted the North Persian concession by the Persian Cabinet.[12] On the one hand, this new element in the Anglo-American petroleum war was bound to make the differences even greater and the animosities even sharper; on the other hand, it pointed the way to a solution. Once again, therefore, Sir John Cadman shipped to New York, this time as "technical adviser" of the Anglo-Persian Company. Practically, nevertheless, he was also the representative of the British government.

The Standard's concession in Persia made possible a "give and take" arrangement. Sir John could now come to the Standard Oil with a very definite suggestion: if the American firm permitted the Anglo-Persian Company a share in the North Persian concession, the

---

[12] The Persian Parliament ratified this concession in November, 1921.

Anglo-Persian would resign part of its participation in the Mesopotamian and Palestinian fields to the Standard Oil. This was the "50-50 deal" which finally settled the big oil struggle and cleared the Anglo-American horizon of war clouds. It sounds very simple and it can be told in a few words, but the effect and the importance of this petroleum peace pact can not be exaggerated.

The annual meeting of the American Petroleum Institute, held during the Christmas season of 1921, was ruled by a much kindlier spirit than the meeting of the previous year. At its sessions and at subsequent banquets, Sir John and his American hosts outdid one another with protestations of love and friendship. All was well once more. The Britisher could return to London with the smile of optimism on his countenance and the pledge of cooperation in his pocket. All American objections against the mandates disappeared, and it was not long before the League of Nations ratified them.[13]

[13] Before the war the Turkish Petroleum Company was organised in which the Anglo-Persian Bank held 50 per cent. of the stock, the Royal Dutch Co., 25 per cent., and the Deutsche Bank (Berlin), 25 per cent. Through the joint efforts of these British and German groups, supported by the British and German governments, an oil concession in the vilayets of Mosul and Bagdad was obtained from the Turkish State (1914). By the terms of the San Remo Memorandum the 25 per cent. of the German Bank were transferred to the French. By the terms of Sir John Cadman's arrangement with American oil men, half of the Anglo-Persian's share in the Turkish Petroleum Company was exchanged for part of the Standard Oil's concession in Persia.

In March, 1925, Mr. E. H. Keeling, acting for the Turkish Petroleum, signed an agreement with the government of Iraq, which naturally does the bidding of Great Britain, giving to the company the right to produce oil in Iraq, exclusive of the vilayet

The Standard Oil now proceeded to strengthen its hold on the North Persian concession.[14] It offered the Persian government a $10,000,000 loan at 7 per cent. interest and probably thought that having done so, the goal had been reached. But the second party, Persia, now proved unwilling. Much to the surprise of the entire world, the Persian parliament, disregarding the serious financial crisis through which the country was then passing, on March 2, 1922, refused the Standard Oil's loan proffer, thus indicating that the concession would not be finally ratified. No sooner had this step been taken, than the State Department took up the cudgels on behalf of the Rockefeller firm. On March 17, news despatches from Teheran stated

of Basra. The concession is granted for a period of seventy-five years.

The Turkish Petroleum Company now consists of four groups: the Anglo-Persian with 25 per cent. participation, the Royal-Dutch with 25 per cent. participation, the Compagnie Française des Petroles which includes sixty-seven French companies and controls 25 per cent. of the stock, and finally seven American firms, one of which is the Standard Oil and most of which are Standard Oil subsidiaries. The concessions contract stipulates that the president of the Turkish Petroleum Company is always to be an Englishman. It is stated that the combined capital of the company is equal to 1,000 million English pounds. Authorities are of the opinion that owing to political difficulties, to geographic and climatic conditions, and to the necessity of constructing a railroad, as well as of laying a pipe-line to some Mediterranean port, it will be seven or eight years before production on a commercial scale commences in Mosul.

[14] "When Sir John Cadman, representative of the Anglo-Persian Company (Ltd.), visited the United States in 1921, an agreement was reached with the Standard Oil Company of New Jersey whereby the Standard Oil Company of New Jersey and the Anglo-Persian Company (Ltd.) submitted a proposal to the Persian government that these two companies be granted a joint concession to the undeveloped oil-fields of Northern Persia." U. S. A. Federal Trade Commission's *Report on Foreign Ownership in the Petroleum Industry,* February, 1923, p. 63.

that the American diplomatic agent there had, on instructions from his government, made protest to the Persian government against its violation of the so-called and convenient "open-door" principle. But the Persians remained adamant.

What was the cause of this quite unusual stand of the Teheran cabinet? The explanation was clearly set forth on February 21, 1924, in a recapitulatory note sent by Hussein Ali, the Persian minister in Washington, to Secretary of State Hughes. After discussing the preliminary negotiations between W. Morgan Shuster, the fiscal agent of the Teheran government in the United States and the Standard Oil in New Jersey, the document proceeds as follows:

"After consideration in the Committee of the Whole, the Medjhelis passed a resolution approving the granting of a concession for the North Persian oil-fields to the Standard Oil Company of New Jersey, and laid down certain conditions intended to safeguard the public interest, among which may be mentioned the condition that the Standard Oil Company of New Jersey should not, in any circumstances, assign or transfer this concession or enter into partnership without the approval of the Medjhelis. This condition was merely the enunciation of the fundamental policy of my government that the capital employed must be entirely American. The resolution, of which a copy is enclosed, was communicated to the Standard Oil Company of New Jersey by Mr. Shuster, with a view to ascertaining whether it was prepared, as my government hoped would be the case, to enter into an agreement in conformity with the conditions laid down therein.

"Some months of negotiation ensued, during which representatives of the Anglo-Persian Company, Ltd., approached the Standard Oil Company and informed it of the exclusive rights which the former claimed in the North Persian oil-fields under the supposed Khostaria concession. Thereupon, in February, 1922, the Standard Oil Company signified a desire to associate itself in the development of the Persian oil-fields on a fifty-fifty basis with the Anglo-Persian Company. Although I repeatedly requested it, I was never able to obtain from the Standard Oil Company a copy of its agreement with the Anglo-Persian Company or any information as to its scope. Nevertheless, I was certain that an association of this kind would be distasteful to my government, and the Standard Oil Company was so advised by me. That company, however, was insistent that this was the only plan upon which it would enter into the proposed concession, and a new draft agreement was drawn up on this basis in February, 1922, and forwarded to my government for consideration. This February proposal was rejected because of the association with the Anglo-Persian Company. On account of this association between the Standard and Anglo-Persian companies and in order to give the government more latitude in carrying on the negotiations, the Medjhelis, on June 11, 1922, voted an amendment to its previous resolution, empowering the government to negotiate a petroleum concession in North Persia with any independent and responsible

American company. With these broad powers, my government extended the scope of its negotiations and sought proposals from not only the Standard Oil Company of New Jersey, but from the Sinclair Consolidated Oil Corporation.

"At the end of June the Standard Oil Company indicated its willingness to conform to the resolution of the Medjhelis and to take and operate the concession entirely on its own account without entering into partnership with any other company so far as the carrying out of the concession was concerned. This new attitude of the Standard Oil Company, which, it will be observed, left out of consideration entirely any partnership alliance with the Anglo-Persian Company, was set forth in an initialed memorandum of June 30, 1922, a copy of which is herewith enclosed. At the same time my government was receiving proposals from the Sinclair Consolidated Oil Corporation through its representative in Teheran. Also after the receipt of the June memorandum my government sought more definite terms, in conformity therewith, from the Standard Oil Company, and a draft concession was forwarded to Teheran in the following August. With the Standard and the Sinclair proposals in hand, my government, in view of the great importance of the concession and the vital interests involved, sought the views of the Medjhelis by laying both proposals before a special committee of that body.

"After a thorough examination by this committee and by my government, the Standard declining to make any substantial modifications in their proposal or to send a representative to Teheran to discuss the matter directly with the government, both sets of proposals were rejected because they did not seem to safeguard sufficiently the interests of Persia. In view of this, the Medjhelis deemed it best to pass a law laying down in greater detail the basis of a concession which my government was authorised to grant to any independent and reputable American concern that might show interest in the matter. The Standard Oil Company of New Jersey did not show any inclination to meet the requirements of the law and made no proposals, but the Sinclair Consolidated Oil Corporation submitted terms following closely the conditions laid down in the Oil Law. The Standard manifesting no further interest in the concession, an agreement was consequently signed last December by the government and the Sinclair representative in Teheran subject to the ratification of the Medjhelis, as the Sinclair Company was the only applicant in the field.

"Now that there is at last a prospect of the northern oil-fields of Persia being developed under purely American auspices, the Standard Oil Company of New Jersey advances certain claims on the basis of association with the Anglo-Persian Oil Company, Ltd., in the so-called Khostaria concessions.

"I need not repeat the arguments laid in detail before Your Excellency in my note of January 3, 1922, which to your judicial mind will, I am sure, carry conviction that these so-called concessions are null and void. If the Standard Oil Company believed it had acquired any valid rights under these alleged concessions by virtue of association with the Anglo-Persian Company, why did it continue for two years to negotiate for a new concession with the Persian Government? The negotiation indicates the doubtful sincerity of the claims now advanced by the Standard Oil Company.

"I can not, therefore, but express surprise that a large American corporation should, in these circumstances, ally itself with a policy known by it to be repugnant to the Persian nation and openly declare that it maintains its so-called rights under the Khostaria concessions and that it proposes to enforce them in defiance of the Persian government.

"The Standard Oil made the mistake of yielding to the unwarranted contentions of the Anglo-Persian Oil Company. They were repeatedly warned by Mr. Shuster and myself of the strong feeling of suspicion inevitably entertained in Teheran, in view of past experiences, as to British motives and aims and of the decision of the Persian government to stand on the firm ground of the invalidity of the alleged Khostaria concessions. In spite of this warning, the Standard Oil Company made their proposal of February, 1922, to exploit the five northern provinces in association with the Anglo-Persian Oil Company on a fifty-fifty basis. . . ."

The Soviet government shared and supported the views of Teheran as enunciated in this note. The identification of the Standard Oil with the Anglo-Persian made the former as unacceptable to Soviet Russia as the latter. Even in the pre-petroleum era, when oil was not yet the world's greatest lubricant and irritant,

Russia's traditional policy aimed to keep Britain at a distance from the Caspian because any English advance towards that inland sea would have endangered her hegemony in the Caucasus and in Central Asia. Therefore the century-old rivalry between the Czar and His Majesty in the Near-Middle East, and therefore the temporary armistice as laid down in the treaty of 1907. The advent of the present oil age made the necessity of such a policy all the more cogent, for the British were far from indifferent to the liquid wealth of Baku and Grosni. Between 1918 and 1920, when Soviet Russia was engaged in Civil War, British ministers and British oil men took no pains to disguise their designs on the Caucasus where within a radius of some 300 miles lies the earth's richest compact oil district. And a concession to an English company or to a British-American combine would inevitably have brought British influence right up to the Russian border, where it would have become a base for intrigue and the sowing of unrest, and ultimately for a possible effort to detach the Caucasus from Central Russia. At least so the Russians viewed the matter.

For this reason and by virtue of the right arising out of Article No. 13 of the Soviet-Persian treaty, the Bolshevik government entered its protests against the Standard Oil concession no sooner had the Cadman peace of New York become known. To the Standard Oil alone the Soviets would have had no particular objection. When, however, it joined hands with the Anglo-Persian, it became as *non grata* as the British.

Despite the Persian government's unequivocal rebuff,

both the Standard Oil and the Anglo-Persian continued to press this case and to mobilise on this behalf certain reactionary forces of the population of the country. By this time, as we have noted, the Sinclair Exploration Company of America was also in the field for the concession.

Harry F. Sinclair entered the North Persian race at the suggestion of the United States Secretary of Commerce, Hoover. He did so after the Standard Oil had obtained its concession and before there could have been any thought of its cancellation.[15]

There is much unexplained mystery in this action

[15] On May 3, 1922, Mr. A. C. Veatch, vice-president of the Sinclair Exploration Co., sent the following letter from his New York office to the Federal Trade Commission in Washington:

"Gentlemen: In July of 1921, following up a suggestion of the Secretary of Commerce, the Sinclair Company began its negotiations with the Persian authorities for an oil concession over the five northern provinces, which are stated by the Persian government to be free from any prior claim.

"These negotiations have been continued up to the present date, during which period the Sinclair Company has had active opposition from a combination of interests of the Standard Oil Company of New Jersey and the Anglo-Persian Company of London. . . .

"To refer again to the competition the Sinclair Company has encountered in endeavouring to obtain this concession, we wish to state that early in 1921 an oil concession over the area referred to was signed between the Persian government and the Standard Oil Company, but in order to become legal this required the ratification of the Persian Parliament.

"While this ratification was pending, Sir John Cadman, a director of the Anglo-Persian Co., of London, came to the United States and while there entered into an agreement with the Standard Oil Company of New Jersey to share on a 50-50 basis with the latter company, the Persian concession when obtained. The fact of this agreement was given to the press by the parties concerned.

"Public knowledge of this agreement in Persia where the desire of the government and of the people is to obtain purely American capital, was sufficient to make the Parliamentary ratification of the contract signed by the Persian cabinet impossible."

of the Department of Commerce which becomes even
more intriguing in view of the support given the
Standard Oil by the Department of State. In this
connection it may be remarked that Dr. Millspaugh,
the American Financial Adviser of the Persian government, subsequently had frequent clashes on the concession question with Rabbi Kornfeld, the United States
Minister in Teheran. Dr. Millspaugh went to Persia
in 1922. Between 1920 and 1922 the *Financial Adviser* had been the *petroleum* expert of the State Department in Washington. Whose interests he favoured,
we may, therefore, conjecture. Rumour has it that the
friction between Millspaugh and Kornfeld ultimately
caused the retirement of the latter, who was inclined to
support Sinclair.

Be that as it may, and the point cries for clarification
we find Sinclair on the offensive in Persia throughout
the latter half of 1921 and the whole of 1922. Like the
Standard Oil and the Anglo-Persian, he tried to win the
support of political parties,[16] and apparently succeeded, for on June 10, 1923, the Medjhelis passed a
law which virtually annulled the Standard Oil concession and had the effect of offering the North Persian

[16] Sinclair's agents also attempted to mobilise the powerful
support of the Soviet government on their company's behalf.
To this end they frequently approached Ambassador Rothstein
who was then in Teheran. With reference to this requested assistance, Mr. Rothstein recently wrote to me as follows: "This
was not refused but not actively given because of the absence
of relations with the United States and the attitude of Rabbi
Kornfeld, who refused to have personal relations with me, he
then being under British influence. Contrast this with the attitude of his Belgian colleague who was on terms of friendship
with me despite the fact that his country had not established
relations with Soviet Russia."

field to any other independent American, and only American company. Sinclair now had a clear road.

Things do not happen quickly in a country like Persia. The orientals like to haggle. Leaders of contending political factions like to have their bribes. In the end, however, Sinclair was victorious, and on December 20, 1923, the Persian government signed a preliminary agreement with his company, granting it a non-transferable concession conditioned upon a loan of $10,000,000 to the depleted exchequer of the Persian state.

Here the famous Teapot Dome scandal intervened. Sinclair's credit in the United States fell. Moreover, certain interested groups were not slow in spreading the damaging evidence brought to light by the Senate investigation in Washington throughout the length and breadth of Persia, only, of course, to do harm to Sinclair's reputation. On January 15, 1924, just about the time when the story of Mr. Sinclair's $100,000 bribe to Secretary of Interior Fall became known in America, one Teheran paper charged that Harry F. had given the Persian prime minister a bribe of $275,000. The charge was naturally denied, but it gained currency and certainly did not advance Sinclair's cause.

It seems that listless, intermittent discussions between Sinclair representatives and the Teheran authorities did take place late in 1924, but no definite decision was reached, either as regards the concessions or the loan.

During this lull, Japanese commercial agents, who, it is supposed, were closely related to the Japanese government, appeared on the Persian scene. The diplomatic correspondent of the London *Daily Telegraph* thereupon constructed a hypothesis according to which "the difficulties which have arisen over the North Persian oil concessions, originally promised to the Sinclair syndicate, will eventually prove to Japan's advantage." The gentleman's guess, however, was wrong; nothing further has been heard of the matter.

Recently the French, too, have entered the arena. French capitalists approached the Persian government with the following interesting proposal: they would organise an international consortium of financiers in which the citizens of no country might acquire more than 20 per cent. of the shares. This consortium would advance Persia $50,000,000 for railroad construction on condition, according to *Mekhsher*, the Persian paper which publishes these facts, that the Persian government grant it a concession to the North Persian oilfields. The Persian state would receive 20 per cent. of the net profits of the oil enterprise, but three-fourths of this income would be used to pay off the loan.

It is impossible now to say what chances of success this French-sponsored consortium scheme may have. If, as is very likely, it is in some way allied with British capital or with the Standard Oil banks in France, it will certainly encounter the same obstacles which nullified the many efforts of the Anglo-Persian and Standard Oil in North Persia. For the time being, however, it is in the market together with the Sinclair Company.

There is no question that before his Teapot Dome scandal Sinclair had the inside track at Teheran, especially so since the Russians were not unfavourably disposed towards him. It seems that in 1924 the Persians were prepared to grant Sinclair the concession even should they have to forego the loan for the time being. But it was just at that period when the American "independent" was busy losing his independence. Beginning with 1925, reports commenced filtering into the Russian press to the effect that the Sinclair Company was negotiating a merger with its old, deadly rival, Standard Oil. And before several months had passed, the Moscow authorities were convinced that actually there was no longer a Sinclair Exploration Co.; that, in fact, if not officially, Sinclair had amalgamated with Rockefeller. Whether or not this will be denied by the parties concerned is not to the point. It suffices that the Bolsheviks believe it as true and are acting on the assumption. When Standard Oil joined hands with the Anglo-Persian, it incurred the veto of the Soviet government and the opposition of the Persian centralist-nationalists. Now that Sinclair had allied himself with Standard Oil, he arrayed the same forces against his company. And unless Russian influence in Persia declines to nothing, which is quite unlikely, in view of the growing strength of the nationalist party under the leadership of the new Shah, Riza Khan, who has always had the moral assistance and encouragement of the Bolsheviks, and who feels that he needs Russian aid to withstand British pressure against him, Sinclair has as little chance as the Standard Oil and as the Anglo-Persian ever to obtain title to the invaluable North Persian oil-fields. Certain it is that the Bolsheviks can not change the geography of the Near East which involves the passage of North Persian oil through the Russian Caucasus, or that they will ever renounce the political confirmation of this natural condition as stated in the Russo-Persian treaty of 1921. Thus "Irandust", writing on April 16, 1925, in the official Communist press in Moscow, declares categorically that "it is absolutely clear that petroleum concessions in North Persia, all of which come under the ruling of Article 13 (of the Russo-Persian agreement), will remain a dead letter in case the Soviet government fails to agree to them."

Of late the Persians themselves seem to have struck upon one solution of the problem. In March a group of Persian business men and high officials, including Riza Khan, who was then still premier, organised a stock company with a capital of 2,000,000 kran (approximately $180,000) for the purpose of exploiting oil in Ghilan, one of the five northern provinces whose centres are the Caspian port of Enzeli and the city of Resht. In all probability this company will merely supply part of the domestic needs of North Persia itself, for, despite the millions of tons of oil mined in South Persia, the difficulties of transportation between the south and the north have heretofore made the north dependent on petroleum products imported from Russia. Should the exploitation of the fields become more intensive, the oil will, for all practical purposes, be Russian oil, refined in Russian refineries and carried across Russian territory to a Russian port through a Russian pipe-line or on Russian railways. Indeed this very eventuality must depend largely on the amount of capital which Russia can spare for it, for at present it appears quite unlikely that the North Persian fields will be opened to the enterprise of any countries other than Russia and Persia. It seems hardly possible that the overthrow of the Kadjar dynasty and the establishment of the Pehlevi line by Riza Khan should add to the available alternatives.

CONCLUSION

THE essential determinant in Soviet Russia's oil policy is her economic strength. The reception accorded to concession seekers and to prospective wholesale purchasers depends, to an extremely great extent, on the prosperity of the country. The last four years have, therefore, witnessed a radical change of policy. "The days of Genoa and The Hague are gone forever," one writer in the official *Trade and Industrial Gazette* puts it.

Exhausted by famine, civil war and blockade, the Soviets were ready, in 1922, to conclude almost any bargain that would give them immediate relief even though it might ultimately redound to the detriment of the nation. Now these compelling circumstances are "gone forever".

"Foreign capital," the writer continues, "can invest profitably in the Soviet Union. But anyone who imagines that we will surrender even the minutest achievement of the revolution or infringe upon our own economic interests for the sake of attracting foreign capital is grossly mistaken."

Succinctly stated in these two sentences is Moscow's concessions and oil exports policy. Oil men may be too busy for regrets but if they had time they would be well advised to mourn the passing of the days of Genoa and The Hague, for had they grasped the opportunity then offered them they might now have been in control of the Russian petroleum industry.

Even in this late year of 1926 there are still to be found oil companies which have not learned the lesson of Genoa and The Hague. They are waiting for the hour when the Bolsheviks will be forced by necessity to bow the knee to them. But they ought to know better. For the longer these companies and other industrialists and governments, too, delay in settling their difficulties with the Soviet Republics the harder will be the bargain which the Bolsheviks will drive. As the months roll by, and as the bankrupt days of 1921 recede further into the distance, the greater grows the confidence and the stiffer the backs of the Bolsheviks. The records of history will show that demands to which they were ready to accede in 1923 were resisted in 1924, and conditions which they were prepared to accept in 1925 were summarily rejected in 1926.

From 1918 to 1922 and even on through 1923 Russia's oil resources brought one attack after the other. First the imperialist governments sent armies to the Caucasus and Sakhalien. Then they thwarted every attempt to settle the Russian "question" in conference. Finally "Big Business" frankly showed its hand. It placed obstacles in the way of recognition, tried to boycott Russian oil, inspired Creditors' Associations to agitate against Moscow, and subsidised Menshevik uprisings in Georgia. As a result, Russia's petroleum wealth was for years a liability to Soviet diplomacy. Moscow's relations to Washington would long ago have been more friendly than they are today had there been no petroleum resources at Baku to which the Standard Oil laid claim. Japanese recognition would have been granted earlier and events in the Far East would have shaped themselves differently were it not for the fact that the champions of the Nippon navy and the aggressive vanguard of Japanese industrialism preferred to own rather than to rent the oil-fields of North Sakhalien. The Anglo-Soviet Treaty of 1924 may never have been scrapped had not the Royal Dutch-Shell inspired the British creditors to oppose the agreement because it may have prejudiced the Shell's possibility of regaining title to its former holdings in the Caucasus. These and many other difficulties on Russia's road to rehabilitation might never have arisen but for the world's need of Russian oil.

Oil Imperialism was a curse which dogged the Bolsheviks wherever they went, and surrounded them with enmity, obloquy and obstruction when they sought peace, commercial relations and understanding.

In the beginning the petroleum trusts hid in the background while their governments acted on their behalf. Subsequently, however, the relative positions changed and we find the companies in the forefront. Yet they invariably assured themselves in advance of the steadfast support of the cabinets of their countries.

Genoa remains the outstanding example of government interference in the interests of private enterprise. Colonel Boyle, the Shell agent, first met Krassin with Curzon's letter of introduction. Austen Chamberlain informed the House of Commons that the Royal Dutch-Shell was courting a concession in the Caucasus with the knowledge and consent of His Majesty's Ministers. The conference revolved around the question of this concession, and throughout the proceedings Lloyd George and his associates fought the battle of Messrs. Deterding, Walter Samuel and Waley Cohen, etc. On the other hand, the American ambassador, Mr. Child, openly played the game of the Standard Oil Company. So did the French and Belgian governments. The Hague was but a repetition with minor variations. Officially it was a tug-of-war between states. Actually the diplomats were the willing tools of the giant oil organisations.

In an honest hour the statesmen would probably confess to these deeds and then deny that any disgrace attached to them. Why not increase the oil resources controlled by the nationals of our country, they could well argue. This is the business of government as much as it is to acquire rich, undeveloped territories, as much as it is to send marines to protect sugar trusts, and gunboats to protect trade in China, or to condition the granting of recognition to Mexico and the maintenance of good relations with that nation on the strict inviolability of the rights of oil companies.

Similarly it was Mr. Hughes, not the Standard Oil, who demanded the denationalisation of properties appropriated by the Russian government. But the Secretary of State could have been holding a brief only for the petroleum company whose legal adviser he was before he entered the State Department and after he left it. For the property of American organisations other than the Standard Oil was never nationalised.

Only the Nobel field and refineries at Baku had been taken over by the state and it was these that the Standard claimed. Hence Hughes' concern.

Likewise in Sakhalien. The billionaire Mitsui interests did not insist at the several conferences with the Russians that Northern Sakhalien would not be evacuated until the oil was leased to Japanese concerns. The Tokio government did the insisting for them. But when the Japanese negotiators had won this point the concession went to the Mitsui corporation.

This close dovetailing between the interests of oil trusts and the policies of diplomats is one of the most significant and absorbing political developments of the last decade. Innumerable instances have been adduced to indicate that the foreign affairs of Soviet Russia, Turkey, Mexico and other countries are decisively affected by the attitudes of the world oil trusts towards them. The desire for expansion into foreign fields on the part of the Standard Oil, Anglo-Persian and Royal Dutch-Shell Companies has and will to an ever-increasing extent put its mark on the international relations of Great Britain and the United States. This is particularly true of the latter nation. The United States must maintain its powerful hold on the oil industry of the world if it is to remain economically independent. And the State Department will have to blaze the way to the oil lands abroad which the Standard and its subsidiaries are to conquer. This form of oil imperialism carries the most dangerous seeds of war. For the sake of oil and markets the United States has actually, if not officially, added at least a dozen Latin-

American republics to its economic empire. In like manner the Ford-Firestone scheme for rubber growing in Liberia might have become the first step towards American penetration of Africa. We cannot expect that practical, "business first" America will be deterred by any scruples when the sources of its raw materials are imperilled. The flag will have to precede the oil drillers and pipe-line layers if, within a decade or more, North America's petrol resources draw dangerously near the exhaustion line.

An agreement between the Standard Oil and the Soviet government would postpone, indefinitely, perhaps, the necessity for the acquisition of petroliferous territories by the United States in other continents, for properly financed the Russian oil-fields can easily meet the needs not only of the Standard Oil's and the Soviet Naphtha Syndicate's customers in Europe but also of those consumers in the United States who could not be supplied by the output of California, Texas, Oklahoma and Mexico.

All authorities agree with A. Beeby Thompson,[1] that the Russian oil "industry is progressing and exports of products assuming an importance that can not be disregarded as an economic factor in the world's oil business." Whereas the ledgers of the Soviet petroleum trusts recorded deficits in 1923, the fields are now yielding a sizeable net profit after deducting royalties, municipal, republican and federal taxes, and considerable contributions to the Workers' Social Improvement

---

[1] Address at February, 1925, meeting of American Institute of Mining and Metallurgical Engineers.

Fund. The surplus earnings are reinvested in the fields and make for the steady progress which all branches of the industry have registered since 1924.

In consequence of these developments, oil has become an invaluable asset to the Soviet government. Its exchequer and its international position are favourably influenced by it. Russia's petroleum resources and exports play a very important rôle in her relations with France, Italy, Great Britain, Turkey, Japan and the United States. Oil is destined to loom especially large in Russo-American affairs because the one country is the richest potential producer of the liquid and the other the greatest consumer. Petrol was the mortar of the Russo-Japanese rapprochement. In Persia it adds to the irritating factors which, as long as the British Empire continues to exist, must presumably create friction between it and the Soviet Union. This, however, is an isolated instance. Generally speaking, benefit rather than harm will accrue to the Russian people from the circumstance that it owns and operates, or controls, oil-fields the extent of which is unequalled anywhere else on the earth's surface. The fact that the Soviet authorities are now managing these in a manner which permits of exports in important quantities to most of the countries of Europe gives the Soviet representatives an advantage in not a few of their meetings with the diplomats of foreign Powers. For though oil more often than not clogs the machinery of diplomacy, it does occasionally lubricate it. Or more correctly, its function changes. It first was a tormenting obstacle to friendship between Moscow and

Tokio. Now it is conducive to a cordial atmosphere. Similarly, the position of the Standard Oil was for years the most effective bar to the establishment of normal relations between the United States and the Soviets. But the rapid improvement of conditions in the Russian oil industry and in Russia generally, plus a turn in the world market which is becoming more and more unfavourable to American petroleum interests has modified the attitude of the Standard Oil, and this change is certain to bring closer the day when relations between Russia and the United States will be resumed.

Cherchez le petrole has become as universal an explanation of the tragedies and comedies of international relations as *cherchez la femme* is of human relations. Those who still believe that wars are waged to insure peace or to make the world safe for democracy or to defend national honour are sadly deluded. Oil is not the only casus belli these days, but though its career as a widely used commodity is extremely short it has already caused more conflicts than any championing of Christian ideals. And it will demand more attention and more victims as it becomes more indispensable to every form of transportation and of industrial activity. The menace must grow as time goes on, and the pacifist, with the Mosul trouble and the Mexican tangle fresh in mind, should not content himself with crying "Peace, Peace, Peace" to a world which will not listen because it cannot, but apply some of his energy to an analysis of the fundamental causes of international disagreements and to the organisation of those elements of the population of each country which have nothing to gain from such complications except the opportunity of becoming cannon fodder. Nothing is won by fighting vaguely against war. The paramount thing is to combat the forces that make for war. The oil kings are today the most promising of these forces. By virtue of their vast wealth and far-flung organisation, by reason, moreover, of the pivotal position they occupy in the economy of their nations these "gas" monarchs exercise tremendous political power and can put irresistible pressure on governments and governmental departments. When an issue arises cabinet ministers act to safeguard the interests of a few petrol barons rather than the larger interests of the common people. And anyone in the United States who would dispute the hold of the oil trusts on his government need merely recall the Teapot Dome scandal when it was proven beyond a doubt that at least three members of the President's cabinet had taken and approved of measures which robbed the nation as a whole of great oil reserves only to place them in the hands of a few private companies for selfish exploitation.

King Coal has been dethroned; coal and iron probably chalked the last war to their credit when the guns began to boom in the summer of 1914. Now oil is having its day. We are living in the Oil Age, and Oil Imperialism is in the saddle. The history of the next generation or two will be read in the light of the struggle for oil.

BIBLIOGRAPHY

CHAPTER I

THE WAR FOR BAKU

The Adventures of the Dunsterforce, Major-General Dunsterville. 1920.

Encyclopedia Britannica, vols. 30, 31, 32.

Zum Imperialismus oder Revolution, Leon Trotsky.

Meine Kriegserinnerungen, Eric Ludendorff. Berlin, Mittler. 1919.

"Zwischen Kaukasus und Sinai," *Jahrbuch des Bundes der Asienkaempfer.* Moscow *Pravda,* April 29, 1924.

The Nations of To-day, edited by John Buchan, "The Baltic and Caucasian States."

From Whitehall to the Caspian; Lt. Col. F. J. F. French, London.

La Lutte Pour le Petrole et la Russie; Apostol and Michelson, Paris. 1922.

Mit Feldmarschall von der Goltz in Mesopotamien und Persien; Lieut. Hans von Kiesling, Leipzig. 1922.

Recent Happenings in Persia; Hon. J. M. Balfour.

The Russian Socialist Federated Republic; E. A. Ross.

Records of the Boris Savinkov Trial, Moscow.

London *Times,* New York *Nation,* German dailies of 1918.

Kazn 26 Bakinskikh Kommissarov (Execution of 26 Baku Commissars), Chaikin, Moscow. 1922.

Turkey, the Great Powers and the Bagdad Railway; Edward M. Earle, New York. 1923.

CHAPTER II

THE GENOA CONFERENCE AND OIL

London *Times* for April and May, 1922.

Moscow *Isvestia* for April and May, 1922.

Genuezkaya Konferenzia (Genoa Conference), Official publication of the Commissariat for Foreign Affairs, Moscow. 1922.

Newspaper clippings of conference period in Archives of German Foreign Office.

Blue Paper Relating to International Economic Conference, Genoa, April, May, 1922. London, C1667. 1922.

London *Oil News* and *Petroleum Times.*

CHAPTER III

IN THE ROYAL DUTCH CAPITAL

London *Times* for June and July, 1922.

Moscow *Isvestia* for June and July, 1922.

German Foreign Office Archive clippings for Hague Conference period.

The Oil Trusts and Anglo-American Relations, Davenport and Cooke.

The World Struggle for Oil, L'Espagnol de la Tramerye, London. 1923.

Oil and Petroleum Manual, Walter R. Skinner, London, 1919 and 1921.

Files of Paris *Courrier des Petroles,* London *Oil News,* London *Petroleum Times* and Vienna-Berlin *Petroleum.*

Gaagskaya Konferenzia (The Hague Conference), Commissariat of Foreign Affairs, Moscow, 1922. A complete stenographic account supplemented by a summary of the proceedings of the Council of People's Commissars, July 21, 1922, at which Litvinov, Krassin and Krestinsky delivered reports on the Hague Conference.

CHAPTER IV

OIL BLOCKADE AND AFTER

London *Oil News* and *Petroleum Times* from 1922 to the present time.

Paris *Courrier des Petroles* for 1922 and 1923.

The Oil Fields of Russia, A. Beeby Thompson, London. 1908.

Oil and Petroleum Annual, 1921, Walter R. Skinner.

American Petroleum, Supply and Demand, A Report to the American Petroleum Institute, McGraw-Hill, New York. 1925.

CHAPTER V

STANDARD OIL BACKS RUSSIAN RECOGNITION

Justice or Plunder, Orange Pamphlet issued by the Association of British Creditors of Russia.

Report of Roumanian Commercial Attaché.

London *Oil News* for May, 1922, October and December, 1924, and December, 1925.

Oil Trusts and Anglo-American Relations, Davenport and Cooke.

American Petroleum—Supply and Demand, Report of American Petroleum Institute.

Report of Department of Commerce, December 10, 1922.

Report of Federal Oil Conservation Board.

CHAPTER VI

SOVIET CONCESSIONS

Petroleum Resources of the World, Valentine R. Garfias.

Trotsky's address to German Workingmen's Delegation, July, 1925.

London *Oil News,* July 8, 1922.

London *Daily Telegraph,* June 26, 1923.

CHAPTER VII

UNITED STATES, JAPAN, AND RUSSIA

Official Minutes of the Washington Disarmament Conference, Government Printing Office, Washington, D. C.

United States Congressional Record, March 2, 1922.

Japan Year Book, 1925.

Official Protocols of the Sinclair Exploration Co. *vs.* Soviet Government in the Moscow Provincial Court (March 21-24, 1925) and in the Soviet Supreme Court (May 22, 1925).

American *Foreign Affairs,* December, 1924.

Moscow *Isvestia* for 1924, 1925, and January and February of 1926.

CHAPTER VIII

IN THE SHAHDOM OF PERSIA

Struggle for Persian and Mesopotamian Oil, E. Schultze, Russian translation with introduction by T. A. Rothstein.

Correspondence between His Majesty's Government and the United States Ambassador respecting Economic Rights in Mandated Territories; White Paper of the British Government (Cmd. 1226), 1921.

Foreign Ownership in the Petroleum Industry; Submitted by the Federal Trade Commission to United States Senate, 1923.

La Rivalite Anglo-Russe au 19 Siècle, Rouire, Paris. 1908.

Oil Concessions in Foreign Countries; Document 97 of the United States Senate, being a compilation of diplomatic correspondence between the United States and various countries on the question of petroleum concessions. Submitted to the Senate by President Coolidge on April 23, 1924.

INDEX

INDEX

Afghanistan, 27, 212
Akverdov Oil Co., 105
Allen, Herbert, 31
American Relief Administration, 25
Anglo-American Lena Goldfields Co., 164
Anglo-American Oil Co., 118, 134, 137
Anglo-Maikop Co., 151
Anglo-Persian Oil Co., 39, 93, 114, 208, 214, 221, 225–9, 234
Anglo-Russian Trade Agreement, 117, 239
Armenia, Russian, 23, 24, 28
Asiatic Petroleum Co., 124
Associated Northern Sakhalien Petroleum Corp., 200–3, 207
Association of British Creditors (ABC) of Russia, 108, 115, 116, 119
Azerbaijhan, 24, 25, 28, 32, 33, 36, *passim.*
Azerbaijhan, Naphtha Trust (Asneft), 170

Bagdad, 21, 22, 28
Bagdad-Mosul, 20
Baku, Oil-fields, *passim.*
Baku Consolidated, Ltd., 96, 115, 116, 169
Balfour, J. M., 27
Banque de Paris, 86
Bataafische Petroleum Co., 42
Batum, 23, 25, 31, 32, 34
Bedford, A. C., 39, 40, 64, 85, 152
Berthelot, Philip, 216
Bibi Ebat Oil Co., 31
Blockade, oil, 92–108
Bolsheviks, *passim.*
Boyle, J. W., 40, 41, 52, 60, 68, 69, 239

Brest-Litovsk Treaty, 23
British, *passim.*

Cadman, Sir John, 216, 218, 220, 222
Cadman, Pact, The, 84
Caucasus, *passim.*
Chamberlain, Sir Austen, 151
Cheka, 36 *footnote*
Cheleken Island, oil deposits, 167
Chiaturi, manganese ore deposits in, 81
Chicherin, George, 32, 36, 38, 50, 169
Child, Washburn, 64
Childs, W. J., 35
China, 174–207
Churchill, Winston, 32
Clark, Percy R., 115
Clémenceau, G., 85
Coe, F. H., 116
Colby, B., 218, 221
Costa Rica, 218
Curzon, Lord, 40, 41, 85, 217, 221

Daghestan, 36 *footnote*
Darien Conference, 184
Dashnaks (Armenian Nationalists), 27
Daugherty, Harry M., 156
Davis, J. W., 216
Day, Mason, 159, 161
Denby, Edwin, 156
Denikin, General, 32, 33
Derbent, 32, 167
Deterding, Sir Henri, 42, 43, 68, 76, 78, 79, 82, 83, 84, 87, 92, 93, 94, 97, 98, 101, 103, 104, 105, 106, 107, 115, 117, 119, 132, 143, 144, 151

Dunsterville, Maj.-General, 27, 28, 29
Dzerzhinsky, Felix, 200

Egypt, 31
Emba, *passim*.
England, oil imports, 112, *et passim*. Also *see* Great Britain
Enzeli, 27, 28, 235
Erzerum, 23

Fall, Albert, 157, 232
Fanning, L. M., 10, 21
Far-Eastern bloc, 177
Far-Eastern Republic, 181
F e d e r a l Oil Conservation Board, 130
France, oil imports, 112; oil production, 123 *et passim*.
Franco-Belgian Syndicate, 93, 97, 98, 102

Gadjinsky Cheleken Co., 169
Garfias, V. R., Russian oil resources, 165
Genoa Conference, 14, 38–67, 74, 75, 80, 86, 87, 102, 105, 237, 238
George, Lloyd, 32, 33, 38, 46, 47, 48, 61, 66
Georgia, 23, 24, 25, 28, 29, 32, 33, 34, 35, 36 *footnote*
Germany, oil imports, 112; oil production, 123
Ghilan Oil-field, 235
Goto, Viscount, 178
Greame, Sir Philip Lloyd, 68, 73, 76, 78
Great Britain, *passim*.
Greenway, Sir Charles, 214
Grosni, *passim*.
"Groupement," (*Groupement International des Sociétés Naphtières en Russie*), 94–98, 101–107
Gulbenkian, 107

Hague Conference, The, 14, 67–92, 101, 102, 105, 237, 238
Haiti, 218

Harriman, W. A., 81, 82, 153, 164
Herbette, J., 113
Hoover, Herbert, 130
Hughes, Charles E., 64, 134, 135, 154, 182, 183, 186, 221, 224, 240, 241

India, 27, 28, 31
Inter-Allied Committee of Oil Companies in Russia, 104, 105, 108
International Harvester Company, 91
Iraq, 20, 21, 84, 216, 217, 218
Italy, oil imports, 112; *et passim*.
Izbekstan, oil deposits, 167
Isvolsky, Alexander, 212

Japan and Russia, 174–207
Japanese oil concessions, 187
Japanese-Russian Treaty, 186, 187, 188, 190
Joffe, Adolph, 184, 198
Jordania, Noi, 24, 36 *footnote*
Jugo-Slavia, oil imports, 112

Kakhetia, oil deposits, 167
Karakhan, L. M., 184, 185, 186, 193
Kars, 23
Kellogg, Frank B., 220
Kertch Peninsula, oil deposits, 167
Khostaria, Akaky, 210, 212, 214, 215, 225, 227, 228
Koltchak, Admiral, 32
Kornfeld, Rabbi, 231
Krassin, Lenoid, 38, 40, 41, 44, 45, 51, 104, 157, 158
Kut-el-Amara, 21

Lambo, Louis, 68
Laurent-Eynac, Charles, 68, 71, 85, 102
Lansing, Robert, 195–197
League of Nations, 34, 217, 218, 222
Lee, Ivy, 144–149
Lenin, Nicolai, 23, 75
Lianosov oil interests, 93, 97

Litvinov, Maxim, 38, 46, 76, 77, 78, 88, 89, 156, 200
Locarno Conference, 174
Lomov, G., 10, 112, 142, 206
Ludendorff, General, 25, 37

MacDonald, Ramsay, 116
Maikop, oil in, 9, 172
Mantashev oil interests, 93, 97
McCully, Admiral, 33 *footnote*
McKellar, K.D., U. S. Senator, 220
Mensheviks, 24, 29, 35, 36 *footnote*, 238
Mesopotamia, *passim.*
Millspaugh, Dr., 231
Minckin, A. E., 162, 168, 185, 191
Mitsuibushi Corporation, 198, 241
Moore, Arthur, 30 *footnote*
Mosul, *passim.*
Mussolini, Benito, 113

Nakasato, Admiral, 200, 203
Naphtha Gora, oil deposits, 167
Naphtha Syndicate, Soviet, 111, 112, 114, 119, 122, 124, 126, 128, 129, 135, 139, 140, 141, 143
Nicolson, Sir Arthur, 212
Nobel & Co., 13, 43, 58, 63, 94, 105, 106, 152, 153

Oil resources in Persia, 11; in Turkey, 11; in Russia, 10–11; in Mosul, 11; in U. S., 11–12; in Poland, 11–12; in Roumania, 11–12
Omnium International de Petrole, 102

Palestine, 20, 218
Peace Conference, Paris, 34
Persia, 208–236, *et passim.*
Persia, oil in, *passim.*
Poland, oil in, 11–12; oil production, 123
Prettyman, E. G., M. P., 20 *footnote*

Poti, 24
Rakovsky, Christian, 38, 116
Rapallo Treaty, 48
Rathenau, Walter, 49
Recognition, Russian, by U. S., 109–149
Riza Khan, 235–236
Rockefellers, *see* Standard Oil
Root, Elihu, 145–146
Rothschild Frères, 13, 42, 84
Rothstein, Theodore, 213, 215
Roumania, oil in, 11–12; oil production, 123
Royal Dutch-Shell, 13, 33, 39–43, 45, 76, 78, 80, 82, 84–87, 93–96, 98–100, 104, 106, 107, 118, 119, 122, 124, 125, 133, 137, 144, 151, 163, 207, 239
Russia, *passim.*
Russia and Japan, 174–207
Russia and Persia, 208–236
Russian Oil Products, Ltd., (R.O.P.), 116, 118, 119, 140
Russo-Japanese Treaty, 162

Sakhalien oil-fields, 13, 156, 157, 164, 169, 179, 180, 182–189, 192, 193, 194, 198, 201–206, 241
Samuel, Sir Walter, 60, 68
Sanders, Liman von, 22, 25
San Remo Agreement, 84, 87, 216, 219
Savinkov, Boris, 32
Serebrovsky, A. P., 121
Shidehara, Baron, 182
Shuster, Morgan, 212, 224
Sinclair, Harry F., 15, 153, 154, 157, 158, 159, 179, 181, 190, 191, 192, 193–7, 208, 226, 230, 231, 232, 234
Sino-Soviet Treaty, 184
Soviet Russia, *passim.*
Spies Petroleum Co., 96, 101, 105
Standard Oil Co., 39, 40, 43, 45, 80, 83–87, 89, 91, 92, 93, 95–98, 109–149, 152–155, 160, 183, 207, 208, 215, 216, 218, 220, 221, 223–226, 229, 231, 233, 234, 241, 242

Steed, Wickham, 47, 61, 62, 63
Stomonyakov, D. S., 101

Tabriz, 25
Talbot, Stafford, 115
Teagle, W. C., 93, 131, 132, 133, 135, 141, 143, 152, 219
Teapot Dome Scandal, 156, 160, 161, 232, 245
Teheran, 212, 214, 215
Thompson, A. Beeby, 242
Tiflis, 24, 28, 29, 31, 35
Tibet, 212
Tokichi, Tanaka, 198
Trebizond, 23
Trew, M. H. G., 79, 80, 100, 108, 116, 117, 118
Triple Alliance, 23
Trotsky, Leon, 23, 24, 163, 164
Turkey, *passim.*
Tweed, Richard R., 79, 80, 108, 115, 117, 118

Uchta district, oil deposits, 167

United States, oil resources, 11–12; oil production and imports, 127
United States, Japan a n d Russia, 174–207
Urquhart, Leslie, 104, 109, 110, 115

Vacuum Oil Co., 130, 133, 137, 138, 141, 142
Vanderlip Washington, D., 166
Veatch, 185, 193, 195
Vladikavkaz, 31

Wang, Dr., 184
Washington Disarmament Conference, 182
Westinghouse Electric Co., 91
Wilson, Woodrow, 85, 181, 216

Yoshizava, Kenkiti, 184, 185 186

Zaharov, Sir Basil, 104

For Product Safety Concerns and Information please contact our EU
representative GPSR@taylorandfrancis.com Taylor & Francis Verlag GmbH,
Kaufingerstraße 24, 80331 München, Germany

Printed and bound by CPI Group (UK) Ltd, Croydon, CR0 4YY

08/05/2025

01864362-0008